FINDING YOUR
GREATER YES

Finding Your

Greater Yes:

Nelson Books

More Praise for *Finding Your Greater Yes!*

The book you hold in your hands is the culmination of years of work by Dan Erickson. I have had the privilege of hearing Dan speak these truths through our weekly "Teaching God's Infinite Wisdom" Men's Bible study. Our group has been a sounding board for Dan and our men have greatly benefited from his passionate messages. Dan has lit a fire in countless men and women to seek God's plan and direction for their lives. I know you will be blessed and greatly challenged in the days ahead to put your hands and feet into action as you also pursue your Greater Yes!!

—Rod Handley
Founder and President
Character That Counts

Every person I know needs to read this book! Dan Erickson has brought God's answer and application of His Word to the boredom, discontent, and dead-end street being chosen by most men, women, and families in America today. Undergirded by Dan's decades of experience as the director of a national men's ministry movement, Promise Keepers staff person, and pastor, the book offers readers the chance to laugh, cry, and grow through the practical yet life-changing points and illustrations that flow from page to page. The insights every Christian—particularly leaders—will receive will give freshness to vision, understanding for impact, and a greater tenacity for righteousness as we face an uncertain future. You need to find your "Greater Yes" and read this book!

—Phil Downer
President
Discipleship Network of America

In a world filled with confusion about what is important and how to reach for it, Dr. Dan Erickson has given us a monumental work to help every person understand their "Greater Yes" and how to live a life that will matter beyond today. Enter into this book only if you truly desire to find and live a life that will "echo in eternity."

—Dr. Chuck Stecker
President
A Chosen Generation, Littleton, Colorado

Dr. Dan Erickson is a forerunner. He is a strategic thinker and tactician in promoting the Gospel of the Lord Jesus Christ. In this book you will be challenged to take a spiritual inventory of where you have been, where you are, and where you are going. It is my prayer that you will muse over it, let it simmer in your spirit man, and let its message flow through you to others on the journey!

—Rev. Rick Lindsay
Founder
Encourage Men To Pray Ministries, Inc.

Too often we settle for less than God's best. We set our sights too low. "A Greater Yes" inspires you to higher expectations and outcomes.

—Dr. Jim Guth
Florida Men of Integrity

Dan Erickson is a man who is being the right thing in his Christian walk. In this book he uncovers the real barrier to the authentic Christian life. Understanding who God has made you to be unlocks your full potential. This book is full of wisdom gleaned from God's Word and a lifetime of experience. Perhaps no other work has been written that gets to the core of what is keeping us from fulfilling all that God created us for. Learn these key truths, and you are on your way to living a life that echoes in eternity.

—Chris Van Brocklin
Director
EFCA Men's Disciple Making Ministries

How can you tell if a decision you make will lead to something great? *Finding Your Greater Yes* is about the greatest decision God has already made about you. Use it to dig into God's heart, discover your purpose and join Him in it. Why settle for anything less than God's "Greater Yes" for your life?

—Leary Gates
Bold Path Life

What if men would submit themselves to a Greater Yes! There would be miracles in homes beyond our comprehension. Dan Erickson has put forth a challenge for men to find their Greater Yes and he is a man who has said yes to God on many occasions. I am privileged to know Dan and his heart. As you read this book you will also know Dan, but you will also deepen your relationship with God. After all, God gives us our Greater Yes's. He is Yes and Amen. Dive in and find your yes's.

—Chuck Brewster
U. S. Secret Service, Retired
Founder, Champions of Honor, a Focused Ministry to Men

FINDING YOUR GREATER YES:

Living a Life that Echoes in Eternity

Dr. Dan Erickson

NELSON BOOKS
A Division of Thomas Nelson Publishers
Since 1798

www.thomasnelson.com

Published in Nashville, Tennessee, by Thomas Nelson, Inc.

Nelson Books titles may be purchased in bulk for educational, business, fundraising, or sales promotional use. For information, please email SpecialMarkets@ThomasNelson.com.

Unless otherwise stated, all Scripture passages are from The Holy Bible, New International Version (NIV). Copyright © 1973, 1978, 1984, International Bible Society. Used by permission of Zondervan Bible Publishers.

Other Scripture references are from the following sources:

The Message (MSG), copyright © 1993. Used by permission of NavPress Publishing Group. The New American Standard Bible (NASB), © 1960, 1977 by the Lockman Foundation. The New King James Version (NKJV®), copyright 1979, 1980, 1982, Thomas Nelson, Inc., Publishers. The Revised Standard Version of the Bible (RSV), copyrighted 1946, 1952, © 1971, 1973 by the Division of Christian Education of the National Council of the Churches of Christ in the U.S.A., and used by permission. The King James Version of the Bible (KJV).

Finding Your Greater Yes!

ISBN: 0-5291-2381-9

Printed in the United States of America

1 2 3 4 5 6 — 09 08 07 06

I lovingly dedicate this book
to
Wesley and Gladys Erickson—
Dad and Mom,
missionaries to the Native Americans,
incredible examples of the "Greater Yes!",
who lived out their potential and destiny to the fullest
and
imagined their possibilities!
Love you both!

CONTENTS

SECTION 1
Defining Your "Greater Yes!"

SECTION 2
Discovering Your "Greater Yes!"

SECTION 3
Developing Your "Greater Yes!"

SECTION 4
Deploying Your "Greater Yes!"

SECTION 5
So What? Where Do I Go from Here?

ACKNOWLEDGMENTS

Cathy Erickson, my wife of thirty-five years and my best friend. Thank you for your love and support. I am who I am because of Jesus Christ and you.

Shannon and Doug, you have been a wonderful inspiration to me, thanks for the privilege I have of being your dad. I thank God every day for Rusty, my son-in-law, and Ginny, my daughter-in-law. What a blessing you all are.

Gabby, Kayla, Alex and Dylan, you are the best grandkids with whom a man could ever be blessed.

Gary Mandernach, for challenging and inspiring me to put the "Greater Yes!" into writing.

David Sanford, Sanford Communications, for his expert advice and services.

Elizabeth Jones, for her excellent writing assistance and patience with me.

Debi Stack, whose anointed eyes and writing abilities made me, and the book, better.

Karen Weitzel, for your transcribing ability and gift of translation.

Ted Squires, Troy Reichert, and Randy Elliott, for believing in and supporting me.

Men of T.G.I.W.—Teaching Guys Infinite Wisdom—thank you for allowing me to present the material to you and for your wonderful response. You are all the best!

FOREWORD

I have had the privilege of sitting down with Dan either in a coffee shop, in my study, or on the road together for a number of years now. Many of our conversations come back to the big idea of this book—the "Greater Yes!"

This book is not academic, but transformational. It is passionate and practical. Dan speaks and writes from his heart. And you will discover that God doesn't just deliver you *from* something; he rescues you *to* something greater as well. We believers tend to be like the children in C. S. Lewis's classic *The Chronicles of Narnia*, who find a safe place to play hide-and-seek while they are waiting for WWII to be over. In the beginning, those children had no idea they were designed for so much more. They were designed to enter a whole new realm of living where the Lion (Aslan) is on the move, where there is risk, adventure, intimate fellowship, and a compelling "Greater Yes!" for each one of them.

Many Christians do not realize that God designed us for a "Greater Yes!" as well. Dan has been a huge help to me as a friend and a fellow pastor in believing in me and coaching me to my "Greater Yes!"

Since I have met Dan, he says to me nearly every week, "You are His best; now be what you are." At first I did not know what to think of this statement. After hearing it again and again and realizing that Dan is not just saying it, but that he really means it, that simple phrase has meant the world to me. He has encouraged me in God like Jonathan did with David. I need that.

As you read this book, you, too, will hear Dan encouraging you in God. You will discover or rediscover that God is calling you to a life of eternal significance. You will learn how to think through and process these ideas in your life so that you can become that which God desires and has designed you to be.

As you will realize through reading this book, God has a "Greater Yes!" for you! Buckle your seat belt and get ready to fly!

> *In the grip of His grace,*
> *Doug Brown*
> *Lead Pastor*
> *Lee's Summit Community Church*

For we are God's workmanship, created in
Christ Jesus to do good works, which God
prepared in advance for us to do.
~Ephesians 2:10

SECTION 1

Defining Your "Greater Yes!"

The "Greater Yes!" calls, compels, and propels you to your God-given potential and destiny. God wants to give you the power to break free, plug in, press on, rise up, and take hold of the potential for which God created you. This section defines:

- Why a "Greater Yes!"?
- What is a "Greater Yes!"?
- What do you have to know to find your "Greater Yes!"?
- What is keeping you from finding your "Greater Yes!"?
- What you have to do to find your "Greater Yes!"?
- What will be the result of finding your "Greater Yes!"?

You can live a life that echoes in eternity!

☞ CHAPTER 1 ☜

Ready to Fly!

Finding your God-given potential and destiny!

I once visited a zoo and observed a rare eagle in a large cage. He was created to soar over mountains with wings spread wide, yet there he sat on a branch, never to experience the power of his potential and destiny.

Many of us are just like that eagle. We have an inner sense that life should be more exciting, our work more satisfying, and our relationships more fulfilling. Without really noticing how it happens, we begin to view our circumstances as cages keeping us from true happiness: *If only I had a better job. If only I could break this addiction. If only I had more money. If only I was single, or married, or married to someone else.*

After years of frustration and despair in our cage of circumstances, many of us give up—on our marriage, career, family, life, and sometimes even our faith. We accept our situation as normal. Hating our job is normal. Accumulating stuff is normal. Being bored in church is normal. Marriage without true intimacy is just normal. Destructive behavior is normal. Divorce is normal. The absent father is normal.

But do you know what the scariest part is? When normal comes to mean succeeding at what does not truly matter.

God's Plan + Your Potential = Your "Greater Yes!"

Jeremiah, an Old Testament prophet, wrote the following. *For I know the plans I have for you," declares the Lord, "plans to prosper you and not to harm you, plans to give you hope and a future* (Je 29:11). This passage applies to us too.

In 2004, I lay in the hospital with two new stents in my heart. My heart issue was an obvious symptom of a deeper need. God was calling me out of my comfort zone, and I was resisting. It was stressing me out!

Sidelined from my schedule and confined to bed, I felt adrift. I missed my bustling daily schedule, my ever-ringing cell phone, and my marathon of meetings. Finally, since I had nothing else to do, I asked God, "Why am I here? How did I get myself in this position? What are you trying to say to me?"

God clearly spoke to me through his Spirit, making me realize that I was full of fear and unwilling to do what he had called me to do. "Because of your fear and lack of trust in me, you have settled for the lesser over the greater. I have a 'Greater Yes!' for you." It radiated in my heart that I would never find true fulfillment and potential until I started living God's "Greater Yes!" for me. This meant I had to stop clinging to the security of a regular paycheck, give up my position on the church staff, and move to a promised land infested with giants. He was calling me off my map onto his compass.

One of Paul's letters underscored God's call to me.

> *Whatever God has promised gets stamped with the Yes of Jesus. In him, this is what we preach and pray, the great Amen. God's Yes and our Yes together, gloriously evident. God affirms us, making us a sure thing in Christ, putting his Yes within us. By his Spirit he has stamped us with his eternal pledge—a sure beginning of what he is destined to complete.*
>
> 2 Co 1:20-22, MSG

Many "Lesser Yeses" vs. One "Greater Yes!"

I don't claim to know your exact story, but I can probably tell you what is holding you back from reaching God's potential for your life—being stuck in a series of lesser yeses. What do I mean by that? A lesser yes is giving current circumstance power to determine your destiny.

- Lesser Yes: I'll keep going to a job that frustrates and drains me.
- **Greater Yes: I'll find a calling that will propel me to my potential.**
- Lesser Yes: I'll go through the motions of attending church.
- **Greater Yes: I'll find a ministry that fulfills God's calling.**
- Lesser Yes: I'll give up on my dreams because it's too late for me.
- **Greater Yes: I'll learn to succeed at the things that really matter.**

It's time to exchange the puny emptiness of many lesser yeses for the explosive power of one "Greater Yes!"

In short, our "Greater Yes!" is what the apostle Paul called *the goal to win the prize for which God has called me heavenward in Christ Jesus* (Ph 3:14). The "Greater Yes!" can be defined as that which compels and propels us to our God-given potential and destiny. So let's keep focused on that goal, those of us who want everything God has for us.

Where's Your "Greater Yes!"?

How many of us are doing the work as adults that we dreamed of doing as children or even as college students? Not many. We've laid aside our dreams because we couldn't afford them. Or the timing was bad. Or we didn't want the kids to change schools. Or we didn't think we had the right skills, training, or background. Or we wanted to stay near our extended families. The reasons go on and on. Meanwhile, the big dreams we had for our lives fade away. If they come to mind again, we dismiss them quickly as "not realistic," or lament, "It's too late." In other words, life is what happens while you're making other plans.

Frustrating, isn't it? So often we set a course for ourselves, only to veer off toward places we never intended—or worse, come to a standstill we can't seem to shake. Then it's only natural to wonder if we've either missed God's best for our lives or just never saw it clearly to begin with.

I'm here to tell you that it's not too late. God hasn't given up on you. He hasn't taken your destiny and given it to someone more worthy.

Christ did not die on a cross just so we can go to heaven, but also so we could live our "Greater Yes!"—a *real and eternal life, more and better life than they (we) ever dreamed of* (Jo 10:10, MSG).

There is not one example in the Bible where Christ called anyone just to be a convert or challenged them to just change their behavior. Conversion and the changed life are the supernatural results of believers moving to a "Greater Yes!"

What if There Were No "Greater Yes!"?

Perhaps you don't see the importance or need for a "Greater Yes!" Maybe you are not sure God has a specific Yes-destiny for you. That's exactly how I lived before my wake-up call in the hospital. But scripture illustrates to us again and again how critical a "Greater Yes!" is for every person.

If there were no "Greater Yes!"…

- …Noah would not have built an ark when it had never rained.
- …Abraham, who left his people for a wilderness, would not have become father of many nations.
- …Daniel would not have faced a king and been spared in the lions den.
- …Moses would not have confronted Pharaoh so the children of Israel could come out of Egypt and be set free.
- …Joshua would have died in the desert rather than lead the children of Israel through the Jordan into their land of promise.
- …young David would never have defeated Goliath and gone on to become King of Israel and a man after God's own heart.
- …Mary could not have become the mother of Jesus.
- …true disciples would not live to die as martyrs.
- …Christ would never have gone to a cross to redeem mankind.

A Shift Is Needed

For far too long, too many believers have been satisfied with just enough of God to escape hell. For far too long, the church has been so busy judgmentally saying "no" that Christians have not broken free to find their "Greater Yes!"

Without a dramatic shift in our perspective, we will continue to succeed at what does not matter. We will choose the counterfeit over the real, the comfortable over the impossible. The result will be empty, frustrated, and unfulfilled lives.

I am compelled to write because I want to stir people out of their cages of complacency so they can fly—so they can experience the life they were born for and develop into the people they were destined to become.

This book is about hope and fulfillment. It is not about doing God's will our way. It is about letting go, pressing on, and plugging in to the source, the power, and the potential that dwells in every believer.

This material is not "fast food." It is a banquet to be savored, meditated upon, digested, and applied. Consider reading a chapter a day for thirty-one days. It is meant to be transformational, not just informational. My desire is to help you move toward your "Greater Yes!" and beyond. Someone once asked me, "What's stirring your cocoa?" I hope and pray this book will be a "stir stick" in your life. Like fine gold, your "Greater Yes!" needs to be mined, processed, refined and formed in the image of the master designer.

I have purposely emphasized and repeated principles and concepts. People do not always get it the first time around. I know you can live a life that echoes now and in eternity.

The eagle in the zoo had no choice but resignedly accepting his condition, his cage, and his branch. We have a choice. We don't have to remain confused about our potential. We don't have to resign ourselves to being caged by our past, pain, sin, or addiction. It's time to *stir* out of our nest of mediocrity and complacency. It's time to live as the people God created us to be. It is time to rise up like eagles to our destiny and potential! Are you ready to fly?

Imagine the possibilities!

MOVING TOWARD YOUR "GREATER YES!"

1. What is God laying on my heart that is breaking His heart?

2. What condition is keeping me from my "Greater Yes?"

3. What are the lesser yeses in my life that are stealing my potential and destiny?

4. If I had unlimited resources and complete freedom to fail, what would I attempt for God?

5. What have I learned that will help me move toward my "Greater Yes?"

MY PRAYER OF COMMITMENT

Father, I want to thank You for writing Your destiny for me on my heart. Thank You for my "Greater Yes!" As I read this book, stir my soul and give me the eyes to see what You see, feel what You feel, and do what You have called me to do. Thank You that You see me as I will become. Amen.

☙ CHAPTER 2 ☙
The Questions of Life

*What you need to know to find your God-given potential
and destiny.*

I have often wondered why people do what they do, live the way they live, say what they say, and make the decisions they make. A friend whom I was coaching once honestly confessed his confusion.

"I have come to the realization that I have spent a great deal of time just kind of wandering around in my own private wilderness. I live without clear direction. God has been faithful to supply my basic needs, but I seem to keep going around the same mountain year after year, going nowhere. I keep facing the same obstacles, temptations, and giants.

"Even though I have had great success in my professional life and have a wonderful family, I still feel empty and unfulfilled. Even with all my personal success, I still feel inadequate. I struggle sometimes just getting out of bed.

"I know God is my Father, but I am not sure He even likes me. I know I am going to heaven, but I don't think that is enough. When I pray, my prayers seem to hit solid rock. I struggle in my thought life, in my marriage, and I have to say I do not have one close friend to talk to. I have spent my life trying to find significance. I don't know what to say "yes" to or what to say "no" to. I'm confused, and I don't think God really cares. I am losing everything that really matters."

My friend was desperate to find some answers to life's questions. He had been trained in the ways of the world. His business demanded that he draft a personal mission and purpose statement that considered his personality, talents, interests, abilities, and experience. He had set his goals and objectives, prioritized and evaluated, but he still was succeeding at what did not matter. He still lived a life without meaning, fulfillment, or destiny. He felt hopeless.

What's the Problem?

I think my courageous friend put in words what a lot of us are feeling. So what's the problem?

At the end of John 10:10 Jesus said, *"I have come that they may have life, and have it to the full."* Jesus Christ promises us a full and abundant life. Once you have Jesus in your life, you're going to go to heaven whether you like it not. But Jesus was not talking about heaven—he was talking about now. We do not have to wait until we die to experience the benefits of eternal life!

In the first part of John 10:10 Jesus warns us that there is a problem, an enemy, *"The thief (Satan) comes only to steal and kill and destroy."* Satan is determined, by whatever means necessary, to do three things:

Steal—He wants to steal your joy, your peace, and your hope. He wants you to think that your potential and God's love and forgiveness are conditional.

Kill—He wants to kill your impact by having you fit in, not stand out, and he wants you to conform to the godless pattern of this world.

Destroy—He wants to destroy the image of God in you. He wants to destroy your significance by having you think that success is the big house on the hill, the car in the garage, or enough money in the bank.

Behind my friend's frustration and despair was an unmet need. He needed to find his "Greater Yes!" If he could find it, he would know when and why to say yes or no. He could live a life that would echo in eternity.

Christ Has the Answers

Christ came to earth to do the will of the Father: to die for our sins, which involved being crucified on a cross. Yet His "Greater Yes!" was not the cross itself. Ultimately, His "Greater Yes!" was to restore mankind into intimate, personal relationship with God the Father. The cross would become the means to that end, the redemption for all mankind. Christ's destiny would echo in eternity.

The reason Christ could leave heaven and become a bug in His own garden was that He knew the answers to life's big questions: "Who am I?", "Whose am I?", "Why was I created?", and "What am I destined to become?"

We will never move to our "Greater Yes!" until we are able to answer these four questions. What our Heavenly Father says and feels about the Son of God, He also says and feels about us as His adopted sons and daughters.

Identity + Significance + Purpose + Potential = Your "Greater Yes!

Who Am I?

This first question speaks to our *identity*. The average person doesn't know who he or she is. The answer is not found in where we come from, what we do, or what we own. Our identity is not defined or determined by what our career says, what other people say, what the world says, what our bank accounts say, or what our sins say. It's about what *God* says.

In Matthew 3:16-17, God the Father speaks of and to Jesus at His baptism, *"This is my Son, whom I love; with him I am well pleased."* Nowhere in scripture does it say that God ever verbally communicated to Jesus before that point. When God spoke these words to Jesus, what had Jesus accomplished? He hadn't healed anybody. Scripture doesn't tell us He had preached any sermons, raised anyone from the dead, or forgiven any sins. He had simply been a faithful son.

On this day in history, before the entire world, God the Father declared that this Jesus was His son. He looked down from heaven and said, "You are my son." One who had no identity was declared "God's Son." We also are born with no true identity, but our Father declares, "You are my sons and daughters."

When my daughter had her first child, it was without the advantage of being married. I remember holding my granddaughter for the very first time, looking into her eyes, and falling in love with her immediately. Why did I love her so much, and why was I so pleased? One simple reason: She was mine.

Christ may have been considered by His culture to be an illegitimate child since Mary's pregnancy occurred after the betrothal but before the celebration of marriage. However, God says otherwise! "I have no illegitimate children," He tells us that our identity is found in what He has declared about us, not our condition. We are His sons and daughters whom He loves and in whom He is well pleased (see Ma 3:17).

Whose Am I?

This question addresses our *significance*. God said, "This is my Son..." Jesus is not just any son—he is God's Son, a Son whom God loves and who is *the delight of my life* (Ma 3:17 MSG). This is significant!

Fathers solidify the significance of a child's identity. Every person, no matter what age, wants to know that his father loves him, delights in him, and is proud of him. I know I do.

As my granddaughter grew up, I knew I would watch every step she attempted, enjoy every sound she made, and delight in every aspect of her growth. I am a proud "Papa." I believe God our Father sits on the edge of His great throne and looks down at every one of His children, expressing joy, excitement, gladness, and sometimes sadness. You see, if God ever stopped loving us, He would have to stop loving Himself. The reason He can be pleased with us is that He sees us with the eyes of His heart and He sees us as we will become. He sees us complete in His Son. God sees our potential and destiny, and that delights Him.

Some years later, my granddaughter was riding in the back seat, buckled into her car seat. She said to me, "Papa! Papa!"

I looked in the mirror to see if anything was wrong. "Are you okay?" I asked.

"Yes!" she said. "I love you, Papa!" She could have asked for almost anything at the particular moment, and I would have given it to her.

"How much do you love me?" I asked her as I looked into my rearview mirror again.

She spread her arms as far as she could and said, "This much, Papa, this much."

As I sat there beaming from ear to ear, I heard another voice whispering to me—a still small voice that said, "That is how much I love you, too—but when *I* spread my arms it engulfs the entire universe. I love you more than all of these." And I wept.

Why Was I Created?

The third question speaks to our *purpose*. The average person doesn't know why he or she was created. *A Purpose Driven Life* by Rick Warren has been an incredible tool that has helped thousands, if not millions of people. It deals with the following. "Why was I created? What is the purpose of my being? To live seventy years or so and then die?"

I don't think you can really understand why you were created until you first come to grips with your identity and significance. Your purpose flows out of knowing who and whose you are. Otherwise you will still be trying to find a purpose conditional to your own power and strength. Your identity and significance are not found in the success of your purpose. It is in what our Father, God, says and feels about you.

Scripture says that immediately after Christ's baptism He was driven into the desert for forty days. There, His Father revealed Jesus' potential and destiny. I believe Jesus could face each of the temptations because the Father had revealed His "Greater Yes!" Jesus' destiny was to reconcile all mankind to their Creator, and the cross became the means to that end.

Soon after He departed from the desert, Jesus went into a synagogue. There, he read a portion from Isaiah, which declared what He was called to do.

> *The Spirit of the Lord is on me, because he has anointed me to preach good news to the poor. He has sent me to proclaim freedom for the prisoners and recovery of sight for the blind, to release the oppressed, to proclaim the year of the Lord's favor....and he began by saying to them, "Today this scripture is fulfilled in your hearing."*
>
> Lk 4:18–19, 21

Each of us has a God-given purpose. God has destiny in mind for us. Its potential echoes now and for eternity. It reconciles mankind back to its Heavenly Father. Our God-given purpose meets a God-sized need. It calls us to a destiny that God wrote on our hearts before the creation of time.

What Am I Destined to Become?

This question addresses our *potential.* God loves and is pleased with us because He already sees what we cannot. He sees through His Son what we will become. It is about moving into the realms of the impossible. It is about believing that we are part of God's great story and that we are key players.

Each of these critical questions is answered for us in a statement by the apostle Paul. *For we are God's workmanship* [masterpiece], *created in Christ Jesus to do good works, which God prepared in advance for us to do* (Ep 2:10). It breaks down this way:

1. Who am I?—"We are God's masterpiece"—Speaks to our Identity
2. Whose am I?—"Created in Christ Jesus"—Speaks to our Significance
3. Why was I created?—"For good works"—Speaks to our Purpose
4. What am I destined to become?—"Which God prepared in advance"—Speaks to our Potential

Several years ago, I sat down with my wife, Cathy. She had walked with me in ministry, followed me, and supported me, and together we had just read a book by Bruce Wilkinson, *The Dream Giver*. I said, "Cathy, I have done you an injustice by not asking this sooner. What is God dreaming in you?"

She began to weep and share a vision she had for a ministry. It was stirred out of the experience and struggles we had with our own daughter who had been a single mother. We realized God was calling Cathy to start a ministry to single-mother families, and it was my turn to serve her. Destiny was born in her heart. It was now time for it to be given life.

Before you were ever thought of, God had a purpose, a plan, and a future just for you. I am continually encouraged by God's declaration to us: *I know what I'm doing. I have it all planned out—plans to take care of you, not abandon you, plans to give you the future you hope for* (Je 29:11 MSG).

There is a good work for us to do, created in Christ Jesus and prepared in advance for us by our Father. God has an incredible story, and He has taken a piece of it, placed it in our hearts, and said, "I have planted destiny in you."

Imagine the possibilities!

MOVING TOWARD YOUR "GREATER YES!"

1. In a sentence, this is "Who am I?"—Speaks to my identity.

2. In a sentence, this is "Whose am I?"—Speaks to my significance.

3. In a sentence, this is "Why was I created?"—Speaks to my purpose.

4. In a sentence, this is "What am I destined to become?"—
   Speaks to my potential and destiny.

5. What have I learned that will help me move toward my
   "Greater Yes!"?

MY PRAYER OF COMMITMENT

*Father, I want to thank You for adopting me as Your child. I want to
thank You for Your unconditional love and acceptance. I will commit to
living out my potential and destiny. Thank You that I am Your masterpiece, that I am complete in Christ Jesus, and that You have a good work
for me to do which You specifically prepared for me to do now. Amen.*

~ CHAPTER 3 ~

You Really Are God's Best!

God sees you, as you will become.

While eating at a restaurant, my wife and I began a casual conversation with the waitress. I said to her, "You know; you are a wonderful person."

She responded, "How do you know that? We have just met."

I told her I believed that God had made her, wonderfully. God does not make any junk.

"I feel like junk," she retorted. Cathy looked into her sorrowful eyes and, with the love of God, shared how special and valuable she was to God and us. Over the next few months, we became a representative of God in the flesh to her.

When God saw everything He had created in the heavens and on the earth, He called it good (Ge 1:10, 12, 18, 21, 25). But when He looked at mankind, whom He had made in his image, He called it *very* good (Ge 1:31). It was as if He were saying, "Yes! Yes! This is now my best." We became God's "Greater Yes!"

You may feel empty and unfulfilled, or you may think of yourself as junk, like that waitress, but I want to tell you right now—that is not true. You are God's best; He loves and is pleased with you, because you are His. You are valuable to Him!

Your Identity + Your Significance = Your True Value

Understanding Your True Value

We make choices according to how we see ourselves and what we believe about our value. If we're really going to be all that God has called us to be, if we're really going to be the men and women, the spouses, the parents, the employees or employers that God has designed us to be, we need to understand our true value.

I don't believe the average person understands how valuable he or she is to God. Remember the four great questions every person needs to answer: Who am I? Whose am I? Why was I created? What am I destined to become?

Our value is found in the answer to those first two questions. How do you see your value? What determines it? What or who do you depend on to determine your true value? What is keeping you from being and doing God's best?

Our view of ourselves is directly proportionate to how we view our personal worth. We often sell ourselves short because we underestimate how valuable and precious we are. There are times we don't even believe God likes us. Why should He when we don't even like ourselves?

Jesus declared that all the law and the prophets are summed up in how we value our relationships to God, our neighbors, and ourselves. He said, *'Love the Lord your God with all your heart and with all your soul and with all your mind. This is the first and greatest commandment.' And the second is like it (equal to it). 'Love your neighbor as yourself'* (Ma 22:37–39).

Most of us have less trouble loving God or others than we do loving ourselves. The passage here assumes we have enough self-esteem to love ourselves. However, I have found that is not true in many cases, leading people to make choices that devalue who they are and their potential.

God doesn't make any junk, yet many people believe and live as if they're junk. When my granddaughter was born to her unwed mother, it would have been easy for people to say she had less value. But I know otherwise. People have told me I will make her egotistical by telling her all the time that she is the best. I just answer, "I don't think so; there are too many of you telling her she's not."

When we understand our true worth, we can choose our "Greater Yes!" When we understand our true value, we will make different choices.

Jesus could say "no" to the temptations of the devil in the desert because he had a "Greater Yes!" and He understood His true value. He had heard His Father say: *"This is my Son, whom I love; with him I am well pleased."* (Ma 3:17)

Myths vs. Facts about My True Value

Understanding our value as God's best gives us the power to say "no" to the lesser yeses and "yes" to the things that move us to our "Greater Yes!" To do that, we need to comprehend both the myths and facts about our true value.

Myth #1: My value is based on what others feel and think about me.

Have you ever found yourself trying to fit in or conform to what someone else wants you to be? I had a professor in college who told me I wouldn't amount to anything. For several years, his words drove and motivated me through seminary as I imagined myself saying to him, "See, you were wrong."

Are you motivated or immobilized by what other people think and say about you? If you let their opinions drive you, you will always be disappointed, because other people's limitations or expectations will derail you from your God-given potential.

Fact # 1: My true value is found in what God sees and feels about me.

God loves us and is pleased with us. We are the apples of His eye. He loves and delights in us because we are His. When we understand this, we will begin to see ourselves in light of how God sees us, and we can love ourselves the way Christ loves us.

The psalmist echoes God's heart when he writes: *the Lord takes delight in his people* (Ps 149:4). *He rescued me because he delighted in me* (Ps 18:19). As I interpret scripture, God says to us, "I look forward to seeing you every day. I look forward to spending time with you. I look forward to loving you, and I look forward to showing you your destiny."

Myth #2: My value is based on what I think about myself.

How do you feel about yourself? When you look in the mirror, what do you see? Too often we devalue ourselves by our own stinking thinking. If we base our value on that, we will be driven by guilt and condemnation.

I had a friend who was always putting himself down. One day I finally said to him, "Why do you keep saying these things about God's creation? I would appreciate it if you would not speak of my friend in those words."

Fact # 2: My true value is conditional only to what Christ did for me.

God demonstrated His love toward us by sending Jesus to die for us—not while we were making it on our own, but *while we were still sinners* (Ro 5:8). On the other hand, Romans 8:1 declares, *There is now no condemnation for those who are in Christ Jesus.* That gives us a lot of hope.

When God sees us, He sees us as what we will become, through the lens of Christ's death. God sees us just as He sees His Son.

Myth #3: My value is based on my achievements and success.

Many people find their worth in what they do, in the position they hold, or in the things they own. By doing so, they actually devalue themselves because they are worth so much more than that. If you lost everything, where would your self worth be? If you could no longer do what you're doing, how would you feel about yourself? You can imagine the problem of finding your value in what you can achieve because you can lose it just as quickly as you gained it. Our value before God, in contrast, does not diminish.

Fact # 3: My true value is found in my relationship with God.

Paul asks, *Who shall separate us from the love of Christ? Shall trouble or hardship or persecution or famine or nakedness or danger or sword?* (Ro 8:35). The answer is a resounding *NO!*

He goes on to explain that nothing can separate us from God's love. Blessed assurance, God's love is unconditional and constant. The result is that we can live in freedom and not in condemnation.

Myth #4: My value is conditional on my behavior, sins, mistakes, or failures.

God does not sit on His throne with a big King James Bible, ready to hit you over the head with it whenever you do something wrong. He sees us through Jesus Christ, so when He looks down at us, He sees finished sons and daughters in perfect completion.

How God values me or loves me is not the objective sum of my behavior or my past. Grace declares that my true value is guaranteed by what Jesus completed on the cross. Period.

Fact # 4: My true value is being conformed in me by the power of the Holy Spirit.

Do you ever feel like Paul must have when he wrote, *I've tried everything and nothing helps. I'm at the end of my rope. Is there no one who can do anything for me?* (Ro 7:24 MSG)? Our answer is: *Jesus Christ can and does* (v. 25, MSG).

God is transforming us, molding us and chiseling away what doesn't align to the destiny He has planned for us, so we can become conformed to the image of His Son.

Myth #5: My value is something I have to earn or deserve.

A lot of us try to earn our way in life. We think that if we can just be good enough, we can deserve God's favor. We need to realize God does not operate that way! I love my grandkids because they're mine, not because of what they do. Of course, there are times when I want to grab them and say, "Why in the world are you doing that?" I think there are times when God would like to do that to us.

Although God certainly expects us to follow His guidelines as to our behavior, our worth in His eyes is not based on works. We could never be good enough or spiritual enough to *earn* God's favor. Our worth is not conditional on our circumstances, our behavior, or how people feel about us. How God values us is based on his unchanging grace, mercy, and love.

Fact # 5: My true value propels me to my true potential and destiny.

When Jesus understood that God was pleased with him and that God loved him, it propelled him to his destiny. You know what drove him to the cross? It was the love of His Father. And the love of His Father was the love of His people. It drove Jesus into the desert, where He began to understand his purpose and where He was driven to His destiny.

Living Out Our True Value

Because God is creating His unique image in us, we can live out who we really are in Christ. The facts of our true value point to one thing: we are His best! Once you understand who you are and whose you are, you will see that you are God's child, and He loves you and is pleased with you.

When I am living out my true value:

- I love myself with the same love with which God loves me.
- I attempt to live out (be) who I really am.
- I pursue God's best for me.
- I determine to be God's best by submitting to the Spirit within me.
- I commit to succeed at the things that really matter.
- I can live a life that echoes in eternity.

From the time my first grandchild was born, I would tell her, "You are God's best." After a while, I did not have to say it any more. I would put arms around her, look into her dark eyes and ask, "What are you?" Beaming, she would respond, "I am the best!"

When she had her fourth birthday, I asked her again, "What are you?" She responded with a smile, "I am the best." Pleased, I told her, "Now that you know you are the best, you must be who you are." It took awhile for her to get hold of that truth. It has taken me a lifetime. But if you ask her now, at ten years old, "What are you?", she simply responds, "I am the best, and I am being the best."

Do you believe the myths or the facts about your true value and worth? How you answer this question will define or confine your potential and destiny. "What are you?" You are God's best—now be who you really are."

Imagine the possibilities!

MOVING TOWARD YOUR "GREATER YES!"

1. How do I feel about my own intrinsic value?

2. Which of the myths about my true value do I struggle with the most?

3. Which of the facts about my true value do I wrestle with the most?

4. What or who do I depend on to determine or define my true value?

5. What have I learned that will help me move to my "Greater Yes!"?

MY PRAYER OF COMMITMENT

Father, thank you for creating me the way You did. Thank You for loving me unconditionally. Thank You that You are pleased with me. God, help me to be the best. I want to live out Your plan for my life to the fullest. I want the "Greater Yes!" I understand that You love me unconditionally and are excited about what I am doing. Amen.

≈ CHAPTER 4 ≈

Breaking Free!

Your condition does not define or determine your God-given potential or destiny.

Craig was raised in the church and has been a Christian most of his life—but he has just decided to leave his wife and two children after twelve years of marriage.

Craig represents yet another desperate person pleading for help. I encounter them all the time. They don't say these exact words, but their unmet need can be summed up in one sentence: "I am stuck; please help me break free!"

Maybe you are thinking, like them, that if you could just change your circumstances, behavior, job, or marriage—whatever—things would definitely get better.

Change is necessary, but change without clear purpose or direction leads you back where you came from. You keep taking laps around that same old mountain.

Hope Born

God has planted the seeds of destiny in the hearts of every individual. We have a hunger for eternal significance. When He planted those seeds at creation, He also allowed us to freely make our own choices. We can choose to accept His destiny for our lives or try to go it on our own.

Jesus promised, *"I have come that they may have life, and have it to the full"* (Jo 10:10b). To my mind He is saying, "I want to offer you a 'Greater Yes!'" He has promised you a life now that can echo in eternity, a life that propels and compels you to our God-given potential and destiny.

A young woman walked up to me on crutches after one of my speaking engagements and said, "All my life people have implied that my condition would always determine my destiny, and that would limit my potential. Today you made me realize that it was a lie. You showed me that God has a 'Greater Yes!' just for me. I want one of those. Can you help me find my 'Greater Yes!'?"

For the first time in her life, she found hope. Hope is always born out of suffering. In fact, God uses our condition to propel and compel us toward our potential and destiny. It becomes the fuel that ignites the fire. She came to understand that her condition does not, cannot define or confine her destiny or potential. We are all cripples in one form or another. God is counting on it for he wants to be strong on our behalf. Only God defines and refines our potential and destiny.

Raccoons in the Attic

A friend shared with me recently that a small hole had appeared in his attic, allowing a posse of raccoons to come and set up camp. Despite the fact that he had a nice, clean house, he was unknowingly accommodating a family of raccoons in his attic. He had to find out where the break was and seal it back up.

What if he had allowed the raccoons to live in the attic? Eventually, the raccoons would have invited all their relatives and friends to occupy the entire house. The man mentioned in the beginning of this chapter, Craig, was allowing "raccoons" to live in his attic (occupy his life), and they were destroying his home, marriage and family.

Jesus described the life of an individual whose heart has been swept clean but whose life has been left empty. He said,

> *"When an evil spirit comes out of a man, it goes through arid places seeking rest and does not find it. Then it says, 'I will return to the house I left.' When it arrives, it finds the house swept clean and put in order. Then it goes and takes seven other spirits more wicked than itself, and they go in and live there. And the final condition of that man is worse than the first."*

Luke 11:24–26

Jesus made it clear that when there is a vacuum in the heart, there will be a lack of fulfillment in the life. If your life is unfulfilled, you will seek to fill the emptiness. If you do not break free *to* a "Greater Yes!", you will never completely break free *from* your sin, pain, or past—and you may end up worse than you were in the beginning.

There are areas in our lives where unwanted things can get sucked in, such as lust, greed, pride, self-centeredness, or unhealthy relationships. Our hearts may be clean, but if we don't allow the Holy Spirit to completely seal our lives, we leave those little spaces open for the raccoons to get in and take over.

Moving Beyond Normal

Many of the critical issues facing our society, our families, our marriages, and our churches can be traced back to a man or woman trying to break free *from* sin, past, pain, or addiction instead of breaking free *to* their "Greater Yes!"

The apostle John tells the story of a crippled man who sat beside the pool of Bethesda for thirty-eight years. Whenever the water stirred, the first person to get in could be healed. When Jesus learned that the crippled man had been in that condition for a long time, he asked him an unusual question: *Do you want to get well?* (Jo 5:6).

If someone asked you that question when you were obviously sick, what would you say? "Well, duh! Of course, I want to get well." But this man gave Jesus the excuse of a lifetime, the one that had kept him sitting there for thirty-eight years. *Sir, I have no one to help me into the pool when the water is stirred. While I am trying to get in, someone else goes down ahead of me* (Jo 5:7).

Destiny was standing in front of that crippled man. Would he allow his condition and his circumstances to determine his future? Jesus was asking him the same question he asks us. In my opinion, he asks, "Do you want to stay in your condition? Don't you really want to move *to* your potential? Don't you want to break free *from* your little yeses *to* your 'Greater Yes!'?"

Jesus was not just asking the obvious. As I understand the scripture, He was asking the invalid, "Do you really want to be the person God intended you to be? Hey, if you really could get better, if you could break free—would you want to?"

What are our excuses? "Well, God, if I had enough money in the bank, or if I had more abilities, or if I had enough education, or if I could get rid of this situation in my life, then I could do great things for you. I could move to your 'Greater Yes!'"

A Man Who Traded Excuses for Action

My father had only a grade-school education but was able to give us a nice, middle-class lifestyle. When I was about nine years old, my dad sold everything—our house, our TV, our refrigerator, our best car—and packed what little we had along with all seven of us into a yellow station wagon. We drove to Nevada and started working among the Native Americans.

He was thirty-five years old when he broke free to follow his "Greater Yes!" He didn't fear failure. What he feared was succeeding at what didn't really matter. His family and friends said he was crazy, but he served on the Paiute reservation for thirty-eight years. He is one of the most fulfilled and satisfied men I have ever met. My dad could have said, "I didn't even go to high school. I don't know enough to be a missionary. I can't uproot my family." But he didn't allow his conditions to *determine or define his destiny.*

As I get older, I understand more and more what God is trying to do. He does not want to just set us free *from* our cages of pain, sin, addiction, and the past. He wants to set us free *to* what we can become. Satan, on the other hand, would like to keep us caged in fear, anger, and disobedience. We can go to church, listen to inspiring messages, and experience incredible worship, but as long as we are not experiencing what God has destined for us to be and do, the devil is satisfied. When we are robbed of our destiny and potential; that is Satan's victory over our "Greater Yes!"

Remember the invalid man's excuses to Jesus? "I have no one to help me. Someone else always gets there first." Nevertheless, Jesus had compassion on him. *"Get up!"* he said. *"Pick up your mat and walk"* (Jo 5:8). To those *of you* who are caged in *your* condition, Jesus is as much as saying, "Get up! It's time to fulfill your destiny!"

Paul exhorts, *I urge you to live a life worthy of the calling you have received* (Ep 4:1). It makes even more sense as paraphrased in *The Message: I want you to get out there and walk—better yet, run!—on the road God called you to travel. I don't want any of you sitting around on your hands. I don't want anyone strolling off, down some path that goes nowhere.*

Your Condition + Your "Greater Yes!" = Your Potential

How Do You Break Free?

1. *Cry out to God.* Acknowledge God. King David in his sin (2 Sa 11), Jabez with his pain (1 Ch 4:9–10), and the apostle Paul, struggling with his past (2 Co 12:1–10), all cried out to the God

of Israel. If you want to know your destiny, it starts with getting down on your knees and crying out.

2. *Recognize that you have an unmet need.* Jabez had to admit he was in pain. David had to confess he was guilty of adultery and murder (2 Sa 12), and Paul had to release his past of mercilessly persecuting Christians to God (Ac 9). Cry out to God and tell Him that you need Him. Tell God you will not be content to be lukewarm and live in the familiar and mediocre. Cry out to God and ask Him to set you free from the cage that keeps you grounded to your world.

3. *Realize that God wants to meet your unmet needs.* God's love for you is based on grace. Grace says this: You can become what God intended for you to be, even when you have not earned it or deserved it. He wants to meet your needs. He's eager to give you your "Greater Yes!"

4. *Look to nothing or no one else to break you free to your potential and destiny.* As I see it, God says, Don't look to your bank account, your ability or a change in your circumstances. Look to me! I am your source and resource. Paul wrote, *Now to him who is able to do immeasurably more than all we ask or imagine, according to his power that is at work within us* (Ep 3:20).

5. *Now ask God!* *Ask and it will be given to you; seek and you will find; knock and the door will be opened to you* (Lk 11:9). James says, *You do not have, because you do not ask God* (Jam 4:2). Ask him and He will show you His glory and your destiny.

Everything Else Is Bologna

I knew a guy who had just moved to the United States from India and was invited to a typical church picnic. You know the kind: bad games and good food. He was late, so he slapped together a bologna sandwich, put it in a brown paper bag and went to the picnic. After the games, the pastor prayed, and the man went to a table by himself and laid out his now dry bologna sandwich. A short, white-haired lady, who had just arrived carrying a big basket full of food, came up to him and said, "Can I join you?"

"Sure, it's a free country," he replied. She put a tablecloth out and carefully took out fried chicken, sweet potato pie, corn on the cob, string beans, hot rolls, mashed potatoes, and warm apple pie. She filled the table up.

The young man was quietly comparing his bologna sandwich with this great feast, wondering how on earth this little lady was going to eat all that food. To his amazement, she gave him a big smile and said, "Why don't we throw all of this in together?"

What do you think he said? Yes, of course! But many of us would say, "You are not getting my bologna sandwich. I paid for it. I made it. I earned it. I brought it. You're not getting my bologna sandwich."

Sounds ridiculous doesn't it? Compared to what God offers us, everything else is bologna. We've got to just throw it in with His banquet. We've got a "Greater Yes!"

What are you hanging on to? What is keeping you from breaking free to your destiny? What bologna in your life is keeping you from the potential God has for you? What condition is keeping you there? God is offering you something beyond anything you can imagine. He has a "Greater Yes!" for you. You can break free! The choice is yours, but the power is in Him.

Imagine the possibilities!

MOVING TO MY "GREATER YES!"

1. What cage do I need to break free *from*?

2. What is God telling me to break free *to*?

3. What or who is keeping me from breaking free to my "Greater Yes!"?

4. What must I, like the crippled man by the pool in Bethesda, take up in order to move to my "Greater Yes!"?

5. What have I learned that will help me move toward my "Greater Yes!"?

MY PRAYER OF COMMITMENT

Heavenly Father, I will no longer allow my sin, my pain, or my past to keep me from my potential and destiny. Show me, Father, my "bologna." Show me what is keeping me from breaking free to my "Greater Yes!" I will pursue the purpose to which You call me in Christ Jesus. Amen!

~ CHAPTER 5 ~

Stuck in Neutral

God desires to see you move out of neutral to your
potential and destiny.

When I was first learning to drive, I turned the car on, shifted out of park, and put my foot on the accelerator. I didn't realize I had put the car in neutral. Each thrust of the gas pedal revved the engine but did nothing to move me forward.

Finally, my dad asked me what I was doing. I said, "There's something wrong with your car. It won't move!"

My dad calmly said, "Son, you have it in neutral. If you don't put it in drive, you will never go anywhere."

If we are going to find our potential and destiny, we have to shift our lives from neutral into drive. We can rev up the engine until it blows a head gasket, and we still won't go anywhere. It doesn't matter what kind of car you have if you never find drive. *The great thing about life is not where you have come from but where you are going and how you get there.*

We can get stuck in neutral, immobilized because we're focused on our past, our pain, or shortcomings. We ignore the redemptive work of Christ that covers our sins, reconciles us to God, unites us with other believers, grants us security, empowers us through the Holy Spirit, bestows us with gifts, and enlightens our understanding. We must remember Christ heals our brokenness, embraces our weaknesses, refines our talents, and engages our abilities in God's eternal plan. Now *that* is worth getting in gear for!

The Challenge

God did not call us so we could remain in neutral. That's Satan's plan. Satan is saying, "Make all the noise you want. Go ahead and look cool

29

and wear that suit on Sunday; be comfortable in your seat; go ahead and pay your tithes—just don't do anything that will make a difference for eternity."

The prophet Elijah presented a great challenge to God's people. This challenge still echoes in our generation. *How long are you going to sit on the fence? If GOD is the real God, follow him; if it's Baal, follow him. Make up your minds!* (1 Ki 18:21, MSG). The NIV says it this way: *How long will you waver between two opinions?*

Today we might say, "Put up or shut up!" "Stop riding the fence." "Fish or cut bait."

The most devastating thing about the question in this passage is the answer—*But the people said nothing.* What a sad commentary on God's chosen people! Unfortunately, that is exactly how many of us live.

From Patmos, the author of The Revelation to John writes to the church at Laodicea, and to us:

> *I know you inside and out, and find little to my liking. You're not cold; you're not hot—far better to be either cold or hot! You're stale. You're stagnant. You make me want to vomit. You brag, 'I'm rich, I've got it made, I need nothing from anyone.' Oblivious that in fact you're a pitiful, blind beggar, threadbare and homeless.*
>
> (Re 3:15-17, MSG)

Near Laodicea, in modern-day Turkey, there were two natural springs—one hot, one cold. People flocked from all over to go to the hot springs at Hierapolis for healing. They used the cold springs at Colossae for refreshing drinking water that came from melting snow and ice. At Laodicea, however, streams from the two springs met and the water became lukewarm, stagnant, and full of bad-tasting minerals, to the point that it made the people sick. Lukewarm, the water was worthless, good for neither drinking nor healing.

So John is saying to this church, I wish you were cold like the invigorating springs you drink from so that you refreshed people, or hot like the healing springs, putting a passionate faith into action, but you are lukewarm like that stagnant water that makes you sick. You make me sick, just like your bad water.

God had a solution to their neutrality and ours: "Look to me!"

> *Here's what I want you to do. Buy your gold from me, gold that's been through the refiner's fire. Then you'll be rich. Buy your clothes*

from me, clothes designed in Heaven. You've gone around half-naked long enough. And buy medicine for your eyes from me so you can see, really see.

(Re 3:18, MSG)

In God, you have all the resources and power to:

- Live your life in such a way that it demands an explanation.
- Live your life so that it echoes in eternity.
- Live a life that stands out rather than blends in.

Lukewarmness + Neutrality = Stuck

What Keeps Us Stuck?

Remember the story of the crippled man in John 5? He had been stuck on his mat, in his condition for thirty-eight years. Maybe you've been stuck in your condition longer or shorter than that, but the question you need to ask is the same one Jesus asked that man: "Do you want to get well?"

Our mat is what we look to for our security and significance. Are you comfortable on your mat? How's that working for you? What keeps you stuck in your condition?

There are four areas that keep us stuck in neutral and from our "Greater Yes!"

Stinking Thinking

Soon after my twin brother and I were born, my parents learned we both had a birth defect. Our ear passages were blocked, and we were incapable of hearing clearly. As we learned to speak, what others heard was not actually what we were trying to say. We could see the ridicule as we became the brunt of many cruel jokes. Even though we were overall quite healthy, that one condition overshadowed everything.

Some years later, after having our tonsils removed, our hearing was completely restored. Although we were thrilled by this miracle, now we could not only see but also clearly hear the ridicule and the cruel jokes. However, the greatest battle my brother and I faced was not the ridicule or the jokes, but the lies in our own minds. We later came to the realization that our value and significance was not found in the words of man but in the truth of God. We could not allow our potential or destiny to be defined or determined by a physical condition. God would later use it to propel and compel us to our "Greater Yes!"

When we allow our thoughts to dwell in fear, doubt, worry, and self-dependency, we get stuck. God wants to transform us first by transforming our minds. Thoughts and words have the power to propel or repel. Proper thinking leads to proper speaking, feelings, and living—which lead to powerful potential.

Paul's words challenge our thinking. *Summing it all up, friends, I'd say you'll do best by filling your minds and meditating on things true, noble, reputable, authentic, compelling, gracious—the best, not the worst; the beautiful, not the ugly; things to praise, not things to curse* (Ph 4:8 MSG). And: *Do not conform any longer to the pattern of this world, but be transformed by the renewing of your mind. Then you will be able to test and approve what God's will is—his good, pleasing and perfect will* (Ro 12:2).

A Hard Heart

This condition is evidenced by disobedience, lost relationships, a lack of forgiveness toward others, and a lack of prayer and time spent in God's word. *The seed is the Word of God. The seeds on the road are those who hear the Word, but no sooner do they hear it than the Devil snatches it from them so they won't believe and be saved* (Lk 8:11-12 MSG).

Recently, I found myself with a hard heart at a meeting at our church. I hadn't spent my usual time with God that morning, and it began to affect my entire day. During this meeting, I started expressing some things that were on my mind—but my heart was hard that day. I tried to ignore the strange quietness in the room.

As we drove home, my wife, Cathy, calmly confronted me. "Dan, you carried a critical spirit, and even though what you expressed was true, you said it in the wrong way. They heard your head, but they didn't hear your heart." My instinct was to get defensive, but I sensed the Holy Spirit telling me, "Just be still and listen," and I realized she was right. I had to go back and apologize to that group and ask them to forgive me because of my own hard heart. My thinking was affected by my hard heart, which resulted in a spirit that was not pleasing to God or anyone else.

What is it that's keeping your heart hard or crowded? We need to give those things up and allow the Spirit to begin to soften our hearts. A tender heart is manifested by humility. It is being willing to go down instead of rise up. A humble person is teachable and listens to the still, small voice of God (see 1 Ki 19:11-13 KJV). Humility tested shows our true character.

Paul exhorted: *Do nothing out of selfish ambition or vain conceit, but in humility consider others better than yourselves... Your attitude should be the same as that of Christ Jesus* (Ph 2:3-5).

A Closed Spirit

The third area that keeps us stuck is evidenced by a quenched spirit, lost passion, anger, withdrawal, and escape. I once heard relationship expert Dr. Gary Smalley say he thought the single most prevalent barrier to having a meaningful relationship with God or others is a "closed spirit." It destroys intimacy and relationships. On the other hand, an "open spirit" is developed through a deep personal relationship with Jesus, which results in intimacy with God and others.

Paul knew that. He wrote: *Don't suppress the Spirit, and don't stifle those who have a word from the Master* (1 Th 5:19-20 MSG).

Is something causing your spirit to be closed so you can't hear the still small voice? That's quenching the Holy Spirit. What in your life is causing your spirit to close? Are the ears of your heart being blocked by your own pain, sin, past, or shame? When you close your spirit to God and others you suppress the work of the Holy Spirit in your life.

The cure for a closed spirit is to turn and seek a deeper intimate relationship with Jesus. I've found that when I seek that deeper intimacy with God through Jesus, it begins to open up my spirit to my neighbor, my wife, my kids, and my friends.

A False Success

A friend of mine, Gary, had spent all of his adult life striving to gain what the world considers success. He had the money, the position, the power, and the possessions. Yet he was succeeding at what did not matter in eternity. He had lost his first marriage and was distant from his son. He had gone to church much of his life but remained a nominal Christian. He was trying to find meaning and significance in the world's counterfeit—and so remained empty and unfulfilled.

When I began to coach him, I challenged him to consider his God-given potential and destiny. He came to realize that he needed a "Greater Yes!" It has been incredible to see how Gary has allowed God to give him new eyes to see through a new heart and mind. He now knows what is real and what is eternal.

The highlight of his change was when he prayed publicly for the very first time at his son's wedding rehearsal dinner and gave testimony to what it meant to find true meaning and significance.

I do not fear failure; I fear succeeding at what doesn't really matter. Paul had a simple view of success and true significance. He wrote: *For to me, to live is Christ and to die is gain* (Ph 1:21). He also said,

> *The very credentials these people are waving around as something special, I'm tearing up and throwing out with the trash—along with everything else I used to take credit for. And why? Because of Christ. Yes, all the things I once thought were so important are gone from my life. Compared to the high privilege of knowing Christ Jesus as my Master, firsthand, everything I once thought I had going for me is insignificant—dog dung. I've dumped it all in the trash so that I could embrace Christ and be embraced by him.*
>
> (Ph 3:7–9 MSG)

The world says, "Find success, and you will find significance." God says, "Find true significance, and you will be successful. Seek after the things that matter, the things that give you true significance, they will bring you true success."

There's a whole different dimension of faith, intimacy, and love that God has for each of us, yet many of us will never experience it. Yes, we'll go to heaven, but that's not *all* of what God intends for us. He desires for us to get unstuck!

Now Let Go!

In the Philippines, monkey meat is a delicacy. In order to catch monkeys, hunters find a coconut, bolt one end of the coconut to a tree, and drill a hole in the other end just big enough for a monkey's hand to fit through. Then, they place some special brown rice inside. Monkeys love this treat, and they will reach into the coconut to grab it. However, once they grab hold of the rice, their fist becomes too large to pull back out.

The next morning the hunter returns to his traps and the monkeys are caught with their hand inside the coconut, hanging on to that brown rice. Of course, any of the monkeys could have let go of the rice and slid their hand out of the coconut, but none of them ever do. They won't let go of that brown rice, so they are taken away to their deaths.

What are you hanging onto that is keeping you stuck? What are you into that is keeping you stuck? What is your brown rice? What are you looking to for security and significance? Do you want to get unstuck? Do you really want to get well?

I hope you are ready to move on *to* your potential. Your condition does not have to define or determine your destiny, that's determined by God. He gives you permission to let go and break free to your "Greater Yes!"

Imagine the possibilities!

MOVING TOWARD MY "GREATER YES!"

1. Am I "stuck in neutral?"

2. What or who is keeping me "stuck?"

3. What would it take to get "unstuck?"

4. What would "unstuck" look like for me?

5. What have I learned that will help me move toward my "Greater Yes!"?

MY PRAYER OF COMMITMENT

Heavenly Father, help me leave behind my stinking thinking, my hard heart, my closed spirit, and my desire for false success. Help me move toward my potential and destiny. Reveal to me what is keeping me stuck. I want to find my "Greater Yes!" May the Holy Spirit show me Your way. Amen.

CHAPTER 6

Rising Up!

*God is calling you off your mat, to His potential
and destiny for you.*

Have you ever been fired? If so, you know how demeaning it feels. I am the only person I know who got fired from his first three ministry jobs right out of college. I made the mistake of telling my bosses that I really didn't know what I was doing, but I was willing to learn.

At my lowest point, I found myself with no job, a one-month-old daughter, a struggling marriage, and no money. During that time, a pastor befriended me and invited me to a conference in Modesto, California. He thought it might be an encouragement to me. He was right!

While I was enjoying the music, and being blessed by the preaching and fellowship, I began to hear a small voice whispering to me. By then, I had pretty much made up my mind that I was done with the ministry. Not only did I have no idea what I was doing, but nobody seemed to want to help me.

My heart was so discouraged that there was no way I could have heard God's voice in this midst of all my turmoil, fear, and failure. However, in the oasis of this intense time with God, I could hear Him speak. He told me that when I returned home I was to pack everything I owned, load up my wife and baby, leave my denomination, and move to Modesto, California, where I knew only one person.

As I sat there, I knew I had to make a choice. I could obey God and put my future in His hands, or I could remain stuck in my pain and past. He called me to rise up to my potential and destiny. And I said, "Yes, Lord!"

That move was the beginning of the rest of my life. The choice I made would echo then and into eternity. That decision propelled and compelled me to my potential. It germinated the seeds of destiny God had planted in my heart. We obeyed, made the move, and were given a "do over," a fresh start.

That crippled man by the pool at Bethesda illustrates where many of us are living. Jesus, knowing how long the man had been in his condition, asked him, if he really wanted to get well. This man had been sitting on his mat, beside a pool, stuck in his condition for thirty-eight years. And Jesus challenged him to rise up, take up his mat and follow him. He called him to rise up out of his condition to a "Greater Yes!"

. *Your Change + God's Cure + Your Standing = Your Potential*

Change Required

Rising up to our "Greater Yes!" requires that we have the "want to," a will and desire to change. I define change as what we have to be or do to live our life in Jesus by new principles, new purposes, new passions, and a new potential, resulting in a God-given destiny.

God wants to do a new work in our lives. We can only imagine what God can do through us when we are willing to change.

Essentials for Change

Change starts with our whole being. Jesus said, *"Love the Lord your God with all your heart and with all your soul and with all your mind"* (Ma 22:37). What we do should be motivated by what or whom we love. According to Jesus that should be God, above all else.

When we ask God to change us, we ask him to change every aspect of our being. He wants to change our stinking thinking into proper thinking, our hard hearts into tender ones, our closed spirit into spirits of openness, and turn the world's success into true significance.

Change is driven by God's grace. Real change, if it's God's change, is driven by grace, not guilt. Change that is motivated only by guilt or shame seldom brings lasting change or life. But grace invites us to become what we can't become on our own. Grace says to us, "You can become the man or woman God has envisioned for you to be."

What God said to Paul applies to all of us. *My grace is sufficient for you, for my power is made perfect in weakness* (2 Co 12:9). *The Message* reads, *My grace is enough; it's all you need. My strength comes into its own in your weakness* (2 Co 12:9).

Change demands faith. Change will require a leap of faith. Faith is the evidence of what we cannot see, and the assurance that God will do what he says (He 11:1). Faith stretches us when God calls us to move off our map and into his destiny. We have our life map; we know where we want to go. The way I see it, our Heavenly Father calls to us, saying, "I want to show you to a new way of living. It's not your map anymore. I want to call you to a different place, a higher level of trust and dependency. You are going to have to believe and rely on Me alone. I am calling you off your map and onto My compass."

Change will always cost us something. We may be thinking, "Sure, I really want to get well." But are we willing to do whatever it takes? There are plenty of people who like the idea of change, as long as it doesn't cost them anything. But it will cost us something. In fact, it will cost us everything. The value of our dream or destiny is what we're willing to sacrifice for it. A lot of people will never experience what they were intended to become, because they are not willing to pay what it will cost.

A rich young ruler once asked Jesus what it would take to have eternal life. Jesus indicated that the ruler should keep the commandments. The ruler insisted that he had kept them since he was a boy. So Jesus came to the one thing that was keeping the ruler stuck, preventing him from rising to his true destiny. He said, *You still lack one thing. Sell everything you have and give to the poor, and you will have treasure in heaven. Then come, follow me* (Lk 18:22). However, the rich young ruler walked away because he had great wealth; he concluded that following Jesus would cost him too much.

A Curse to Overcome

What is keeping you from getting up? What is keeping you from your cure?

There is a curse on every one of us. The curse came through Adam and Eve as a result of sin. The curse keeps us from our potential and destiny. You remember how it happened:

> *The serpent told the Woman, "You won't die. God knows that the moment you eat from that tree, you'll see what's really going on. You'll be just like God, knowing everything, ranging all the way from good to evil."*

> *When the Woman saw that the tree looked like good eating and realized what she would get out of it—she'd know everything!—she took and ate the fruit and then gave some to her husband, and he ate."*

> (Ge 3:4-6 MSG)

The curse follows a predictable course:

The curse begins with deception. Satan questions the truth and causes us to wonder if maybe we misunderstood God. Because Satan will always question God's "Greater Yes!" for our lives, we must counter his deception with the truth.

Deception leads to distortion. Satan told Eve, "You can be like God. You can know good from evil." At that time, what did Eve know? From the moment she was created, she only knew the good. We must counter the distortion with the real, the genuine.

Satan plants a desire. When we buy into the deception and distortion, Satan plants a desire in our hearts. Satan plants worldly desire in us in three ways. *Practically everything that goes on in the world—wanting your own way, wanting everything for yourself, wanting to appear important—has nothing to do with the Father. It just isolates you from him* (1 Jo 2:16 MSG).

Desire requires decision. Eve ate the fruit, and then she gave some to her husband. Adam could have stopped it, but he was complacent in his little garden. He never thought about the consequences of the decision.

Disobedience becomes the fatal step. Their decision led them to disobedience and they hid from God. We know we're disobeying when we find ourselves hiding, blaming others, and rationalizing. When we're being disobedient, we're always going to want to hide from reality and truth. Satan wants you to believe that it's safer to live in denial.

Who are you blaming for your cage of circumstances, your pain, your past, and your sin? Adam blamed Eve. Eve blamed the serpent. The crippled man at the pool blamed the guy who hadn't put him in the water. What or who are you blaming for your disobedience or your condition?

Then there's the discovery. We always get caught. We may try, like Eve, to blame our version of the serpent. But we don't have that excuse, because in Jesus, we have a choice. We really can choose between good and evil. Whether we live in denial or truth, in rebellion or repentance, it is our choice.

The result is either destruction or repentance. The choice is ours. We are being called to rise up and move to our "Greater Yes!" that is found in Jesus Christ.

Standing Required

Rising up will require that we stand. I define it as the ability to live with a godly confidence and conviction. It is the engaging of all of our mind, heart, soul, and strength in those things that really matter for now and eternity. Christ makes it clear that if we're going to rise up to our destiny, standing is required. What does it take to stand?

Know the secret. The secret to standing is we've got to stand on our knees. You will never stand as tall as you are as when you are on your knees. It's not standing in our own strength. It's not me pulling myself up by my bootstraps. I'm not that good, and I know it. But we can't just sit there bound to our mat. It starts with crying out to God.

I've tried to stand firm in my own strength, and I have fallen every time. I still remain crippled. But when I put my hands into the hands of God, I hear Him say, "Rise. Rise to your destiny." Suddenly, through His power I can stand up! I'm empowered to do what I had thought to be impossible.

Then, how do we keep standing?

Plug in! We've got to plug into the power of the Holy Spirit, and we've got to plug into a godly confidence. Having accepted Christ Jesus we have all of the power of the Holy Spirit within us. We don't need more of the Holy Spirit—He needs more of us.

A doctor once told me that we use less than ten percent of the full capacity of our brains. I wonder how much of the Holy Spirit we use. Can you imagine what it would be like if we could plug into the full potential we have in the Spirit who resides in each believer?

Put on! Put on what? *Put on the full armor of God, so that when the day of evil comes, you may be able to stand your ground. Stand firm then, with the belt of truth buckled around your waist.* (Ep 6:13-14).

Take up! Jesus instructed the invalid man, "Now take up your mat." All of us have a mat. But notice that our Lord doesn't say, "Get rid of the mat." He says to take it up. Why does He want me to take up this old mat? Doesn't the mat represent all my past, pain, and sin? Doesn't it represent the condition I was in before I entered into God's cure? And what does He want me to do with it once I take it up?

God wants us to take it up because he's going to use it as fuel to propel and compel us to our God-given potential. It becomes the resource for dynamic ministry.

What is God asking you to take up? Whatever is keeping you in your condition; whatever is keeping you from your destiny, from moving off your map and onto God's compass. Is it fear? Is it self-reliance? Is it your success? Is it sin? What is keeping you from your destiny?

I have a friend, a wonderful believer who has struggled with pornography for years. We are walking through a process of confession, healing, and accountability. He's struggled all his life, thinking, "If I could just get rid of this, then I could do my 'Greater Yes!'" My response to him: No question, God wants to and can deliver you from this sin. But complete freedom will never come until you exchange your sin for the cure and begin moving *to* your "Greater Yes!" Yes, you have to deal with the sin you are facing, and it can rob you of your potential, but it doesn't have to. Your "Greater Yes!" becomes the reason you want to rise to the cure and be set free so you can be and do what God destined for you. Some day you're going to be able to sit down with other men who are struggling with this area of their life, who are sex addicts but won't admit to it. God is going to use it as fuel to compel and propel you to your destiny.

Exchange it! Whatever is keeping you in your condition is the very thing Jesus wants you to take up. He wants to exchange:

- Your condemnation for His righteousness.
- Your death for His life.
- Your bondage for His freedom.
- Your passion for His compassion.
- Your compromise for His commitment.
- Your curse for His cure.
- Your strength, which is weak, for His strength, which is powerful.
- Your fear for His courage.
- Your pride for His humility.
- Your worry for His worship.
- Your success for His significance.
- Your doubt for His faith.
- Your despair for His hope.
- Your hate for His love.
- Your works for His grace.
- Your happiness for His joy.
- Your suffering for His glory.
- Your defeat for His victory.
- Your anger for His forgiveness.

He will exchange your condition for a potential and destiny—for your "Greater Yes!"

Imagine Paul's passion as he wrote: *It is for freedom that Christ has set us free. Stand firm, then, and do not let yourselves be burdened again by the yoke of slavery* (Ga 5:1).

How about you? Will you rise up? Will you take up your destiny? It's really a choice. Our condition does not define or determine our destiny. In fact, our condition propels us to our destiny. It is time to rise up.

Imagine the possibilities!

Moving Toward Your "Greater Yes!"

1. What is God's voice calling me to "move to"?

2. What has to change in or around me in order for me to "rise up"?

3. What is keeping me from "moving to"?

4. What am I depending on or looking to before I can "rise up" or "move to" my "Greater Yes!"?

5. What have I learned that will help me move toward my "Greater Yes!"?

My Prayer of Commitment

Father, I do not want to live my life stuck in neutral. I want to be in gear, moving for You. I want to rise up. Give me the inner strength to change, move into my cure, and stand on my knees while taking up my past, pain, sin, or addiction and exchanging it for Your potential for me. I now know that my condition does not define or determine my destiny. Amen.

↣ Chapter 7 ↢

Life to the Full

*God wants you to have a life that experiences
your potential and destiny.*

My dad started a "train ministry." He has a room at his house filled with model trains because, "Old guys like trains," he says. About thirty-five guys signed up for his train club, and he uses it to share Jesus Christ with them. Even though he is more than eighty years old, Dad is still coming up with new ways to achieve his "Greater Yes!"

My dad has found what a lot of people are missing in their lives—fulfillment. At thirty-five, he exchanged a career for a calling, and found fulfillment. Fulfillment is the direct result of finding and responding to God's "Greater Yes!" for our lives.

Finding that elusive thing that will bring us a sense of completion and personal satisfaction drives us on through career changes, new homes or cars, a different church, or whatever it is that we think will refill or fulfill us. I don't think God cares that much about what you do for your career. He is more concerned with how you are investing your life. The worst thing that can happen to any individual is not dying, but wasting life—making a living but not a life.

My son recently graduated from college. Since then I have been talking with him about fulfillment. At his commencement, someone quoted John Ortberg's book, *If You Want to Walk on Water, You've Got to Get Out of the Boat.* Ortberg wrote the following.

A calling, which is something I do for God, is replaced by a career, which threatens to become my god. A career is something I choose for myself; a calling is what I receive. A career is something I do for myself; a calling is something I do for God. A career promises status, money, or power; a calling generally promises difficulty and even some suffering—and the opportunity to be used by God. A career is about upward mobility; a calling generally leads to downward mobility.[1]

My son and I talked about the difference between a career and a calling, and what it really means to have fulfillment in life. So many, young and old alike, are looking for a career, a way to make a living. But, as I told my son, "You don't need a career or to make a living. You need a 'Greater Yes!' Once you have God's 'Greater Yes!', the career becomes a means to that end."

When I think about fulfillment, I think of completion. I ask myself: do I feel complete in all the gifts, talents, and opportunities God has given me? Of course, your career should be an outlet of your calling, but you have to ask, "What am I seeking?" If you're seeking after position, power, prestige, possessions, and those kinds of things, you're going after a career. But if you say, "I really want the will of God to be done in my life," then you know you are seeking God's calling and potential for you.

Your "Greater Yes!" + Your Potential = Your Fulfillment

You'll never become complete in what you do until you are complete in who you are. Fulfillment really flows out of who you are. Genesis 37–50 tells the story of Joseph, Jacob's favorite among his twelve sons. Joseph went from being the favored son to being sold into slavery by his jealous brothers to being cast into a jail in Egypt—quite a journey! Joseph made the choice to move toward his destiny. He would not allow his circumstances to dictate his potential. As we look at the life of Joseph, we find a formula for fulfillment.

He saw his potential *(Ge 37:1–11).*

God used Joseph's dreams to begin to share with him his potential. Joseph understood the difference between a call and a career. We have an eternal destiny that we don't fully understand until we see the big picture of what God wants to do in our lives. Because Joseph trusted that God had a purpose for him, he was able to catch a glimpse of his big picture, although he probably didn't fully understand it until many years later.

God has a calling for each of us. He doesn't want you to just live and die—he wants to give you a cause, something to live for every day, something to bring you fulfillment as a husband or a wife, as a parent, as an employee, as a mentor, as a neighbor, as a friend, and as a Christian.

He developed patience *(Ge 37:12–40:23).*

This is an area in which I often struggle. I find myself praying, "God, give me patience, and give it to me now, please." Joseph had the virtue of patience, and it kept him going through the circumstances and trials he endured. He was thrown into a pit—by his own brothers—and he had every reason to give in to despair. But through that circumstance God prepared a path to bring Joseph to his destiny. Trials prepare us for our "Greater Yes!"

God needed to get Joseph ready to serve and to lead. Joseph was probably thinking, "How can I do anything for God from the bottom of a pit?" Do you ever feel that way? Do you ever feel like your job is a pit? Do you ever feel like your marriage is the pits? Have you thought, "I'm never going to get out of this"? "How did I ever get here?"

God allows circumstances to happen in our lives according to our need. We might see a trial as a problem, but God sees it as meeting an unmet need. He is preparing us for something greater. He is ripping away what does not belong in our lives so he can produce fruit that will last. *"You did not choose me, but I chose you and appointed you to go and bear fruit—fruit that will last. Then the Father will give you whatever you ask in my name"* (Jo 15:16).

I remember watching a farmer in California pulling eight-foot ripper plows behind his tractor, breaking up hardpan hidden beneath the surface of the ground. Hardpan is a thick, rock-hard clay that's almost like bedrock. From the surface, the ground looked fertile, but underneath the earth had become so hard water could not penetrate it.

The farmer was preparing the ground to plant almond trees. In order for the trees to receive nourishment and have a dynamic root system, the hardpan had to be broken up. I literally saw chucks of what looked like white rock carried off the field by the truckload.

A couple of years later, a field full of young beautiful, healthy trees had grown ready to produce the fruit they were created to bear.

He remained faithful *(Ge 39–40).*

Just when things started looking up for Joseph, he encountered yet another trial. He was a servant in a wonderful home with great responsibility, but his master's wife falsely accused him of trying to assault her, and he ended up in jail.

Although from a human perspective Joseph's circumstance looked hopeless, he remembered who he was, and he remained faithful. If you know who you are, and whose you are, you can stay on course. But without a strong sense of your identity, you're always going to be drifting off to every new whim or fancy that comes along.

When I was twenty-six years old, struggling to get through seminary and support my family, I worked for a successful business. One day they offered me a partnership in the company, and I was faced with a decision. The temptation was strong to stray off my original course toward a life of ministry, and continual financial struggle, and to veer into a comfortable job with a rich company. But I recognized it as a trial God was using to prepare me for ministry. It would have been nice to accept the offer, but it would have been wrong.

Joseph could have just slept with Potiphar's wife, and he may have found his life easier after that. But he was faithful, even knowing the consequences. That's the hardest part of being full of faith—not giving up.

He stayed ready and available *(Ge 41:14)*.

If I were in Joseph's shoes, I have to admit that I would want to crawl into a corner, curl up into a fetal position, and become bitter about my circumstance. However, Joseph didn't turn his back and say, "I've been robbed; forget you guys." The Bible shows us that Joseph was blessed in everything he did because he saw it as an opportunity to complete his potential.

A man I know went through Bible college years ago, but he's never gone into professional ministry. He's a computer genius, and God has given him an incredible capacity to work with computers, but he's never been able to connect the dots to see what he could do for God with his talent. Consequently, he has never felt fulfilled.

You may feel like God is calling you toward a "Greater Yes!", but you don't feel qualified. Take a lesson from Joseph, and be open and ready for God to use you. God does not need our ability—just our availability. He'll take care of the rest.

He grew in spiritual vitality *(Ge 39:1–6; 19–23)*.

If you read the complete story, you will notice that Joseph had a profound impact on everyone around him. By staying close to God, he became God in the flesh to everyone he met.

In order to be truly fulfilled, we have to understand that what we do on earth will count for eternity. Can you imagine what would happen if you invested an hour or so a day in your spiritual walk? How would that change your spiritual vitality? How would it affect your eternity?

Joseph kept God as his priority throughout the highs and the lows. Nothing grows on mountaintops. The fertile ground is in the valleys—the trials, the slavery, and the pits—and it is there that we grow and blossom as Christians. God wants to develop our spiritual eyes and ears and give us hearts that beat after His. That's what Joseph developed, and through it, God allowed him to save his family and the future nation of Israel.

Our complete dependency on God draws us closest to Him. Outwardly successful and talented may go to God and say, "Hey, God, thanks a lot for all You've done. I'll see You when I need You." That's not what God desires! He wants us to come to Him, utterly dependent, and tell Him, "I can't do a thing without You. You're everything to me." Spiritual vitality develops from that kind of a relationship with God.

He became clothed with humility *(Ge 41:15–16)*.

The key to being clothed with humility is getting a proper view of ourselves. In Genesis 37, we see Joseph bragging to his brothers about his dream. He was full of pride. I wonder if God was thinking, "I'm going to use you, but first I'm going to take you through some circumstances that will teach you humility."

Joseph had found a proper view of himself when he answered Pharaoh, "I cannot do it, but God will give Pharaoh the answer he desires" (Ge 41:16). He realized that God doesn't need us to accomplish His will, but He does want to use us. God is more concerned about doing His work *in* us than *through* us.

He possessed a godly confidence *(Ge 41:16–32)*.

Once he had clothed himself in humility, Joseph could have a godly confidence because he understood he could not do anything without God. Not only did he find a proper view of himself, he found a proper view of God. That's how you develop godly confidence. God doesn't want a bunch of wimps. God wants you to go into your job, into your home, into your church with confidence—but a godly confidence, clothed in humility. A godly confidence does not depend on self; it depends on God.

He demonstrated selflessness *(Ge 41:33–36).*

When Joseph offered Pharaoh his solution to the famine, he didn't jump up and yell, "Hey, I'm your man!" Joseph might have reacted that way before, but now he offered his advice with humility and a godly confidence, "Find a discerning and wise man." After being so mistreated, you could say Joseph deserved the position, but he waited until Pharaoh said, "You're the man."

Joseph demonstrated selflessness by putting the interests of others first. He understood that God wants to use us to serve His people and fulfill His will. It is not about us and not about now.

He displayed discernment and wisdom *(Ge 41:37–57).*

Finally, Joseph was able to use the gifts God had given him, and he displayed his discernment and wisdom by stockpiling Egypt's food in preparation for the famine. He lived his new life by new principles.

Too many of us are living the new life by old principles. When we become believers, it should revolutionize everything we do! Joseph used his power and position for the good of others, keeping an eternal perspective.

Nick was a brand-new Christian who had been an alcoholic for many years. His years of drinking led to a nasty divorce. Every time he tried to talk about his ex-wife, he started cursing, angry that his wife could not see the change in him. He had stopped drinking, but still possessed the same anger, stubbornness, and stinking thinking. He was just a dry drunk. I told him, "If you want your wife and family back, fall in love with Jesus Christ, allow him to change your attitude and actions, and give your family time to fall in love with the Christ in you."

He celebrated life *(Ge 50:18–21).*

Fulfilled people know how to celebrate. The story of Joseph ends with Joseph's father and brothers all coming to see him. Because he had chosen to become better, not bitter, he was able to say, "You intended to harm me, but God intended it for good to accomplish what is now being done, the saving of many lives" (see Ge 50:20). He didn't say, "God intended it for good so that I would now be second to Pharaoh." Joseph had an eternal perspective; he saw God using him, through all his trials, to save all God's people.

When we're really fulfilled, we can celebrate. We don't celebrate what we've accomplished, but we celebrate how God used us to accomplish something great in others. It is great to see what God is doing in my own son's life, in my own family's life.

Real fulfillment comes when we realize that we can choose to bloom wherever God plants us. Not, "If I could just get the right job," or "If I were only in the right church," but *wherever* God has put you. Find your "Greater Yes!" and bloom where you're planted. Then God will give you fulfillment.

I never relocated because of a career change. I went because God called me, and I bloomed where I was planted. It's a choice. You can be completely fulfilled in your career, marriage, as a parent, as a worker in your church, wherever it is, if God calls you to it. The result: You'll find significance and fulfillment in what really matters.

Imagine the possibilities!

MOVING TOWARD MY "GREATER YES!"

1. What am I seeking to give me fulfillment?

2. If those things don't matter in eternity, what should I be seeking instead?

3. What trials do I see God using to meet a need in my life that I might not have realized I had?

4. How do I need to change my thinking to develop an eternal perspective?

5. What have I learned that will help me move toward my "Greater Yes!"?

My Prayer of Commitment

Heavenly Father, thank You for desiring to use me right where You've put me. I want to know Your "Greater Yes!" in the midst of my circumstance. I know You want to use them in my life to bring me fulfillment. Show me how I can find fulfillment right where You have me. Please help me to develop patience, humility, and a godly confidence so I can be Your faithful servant. Amen.

SECTION 2

Discovering Your "Greater Yes!"

Seven keys to discovering your "Greater Yes!" will help unlock your potential and destiny. These keys seek to answer the following questions:

- What is God showing you that can only be seen through the eyes of your heart?

- What is God laying on your heart that could only have come from Him?

- What has God put in your heart that causes your heart to break?

- What is God creating in you that could only have come from and be accomplished by Him?

- What is God showing you that breaks God's heart?

- How has God used you in the past and how does He want to use you now?

- What kind of legacy do you want to leave behind that will echo in eternity?

You can live a life that stands alone rather than blends in!

☞ CHAPTER 8 ☜

Seeing What God Sees

*What is God showing you that can only be seen through
the eyes of your heart?*

The missionary life on a reservation has some interesting challenges. One responsibility that fell to my three brothers and me
was to ride along with our dad when he transported those with no cars
to and from church.

Our job was to help the women out of the van and escort them to
their homes. Few houses on the reservations had electricity at that
time, so it was important to make sure they arrived safely.

One winter evening, when a glance at the sky was the only weather
forecast necessary, we tried to outrun a fierce snowstorm. I was the son
on duty that night. We worked quickly, but by the time we had loaded
the people into the van the snow had started. As snow continued
falling, the night became darker and darker, and the dirt road we came
in on completely disappeared under a white blanket.

On our return to the church, the snowfall increased, and so did my
fear. This was no "White Christmas" snowfall; it was a prairie blizzard.
My dad could not tell where the road was; much less where exactly we
were on it. Finally, he shut off the engine, looked at me, and said,
"We're going have to leave the van and walk."

It is one thing to drive on dirt roads in a snowstorm—but to walk?
I thought it was crazy, but I also knew we had no other choice.

As we began our dreadful journey, my dad prayed for protection
and clear direction. I was just praying we wouldn't freeze to death. He
knew that as long as we did not end up in the sagebrush, we would be
walking on the right path. Dad kept trying to encourage me by saying
calmly, "Stay close to me and look for the light, look for the light."

When the church was constructed, a cross was raised on the roof peak, and on the cross Dad requested a light be mounted. He wanted the light to continually shine from that cross throughout the reservation. That light was to become a beacon of hope for those who were lost. I remember one other permanent light, and that was in the phone booth by the only store. In summer that phone booth was always was full of bugs.

As we trudged through the snow I tried to look brave, but I was scared. I think my dad must have sensed my fear because he drew close and put his arms around me. I don't know if I felt any warmer or if it changed the condition we were in, but his arms around me was comforting. He kept saying, "It's going to be okay. Stay close to me and keep looking for the light."

After what seemed like hours, we glimpsed a tiny beam of light from that old cross breaking through the storm. Now my father said to me, "Keep moving toward the light, keep your eyes on the light." I noticed as I got closer to the cross that the light got brighter, my walk got swifter, my body got warmer, and my heart found hope and peace. It wasn't long before we were running toward the light, and as we arrived at the warmth of that safe haven, we laughed with relief and joy.

As I look back now, I am reminded of the following:

> *Why would you ever complain, O Jacob, or, whine, Israel, saying,* *"God has lost track of me. He doesn't care what happens to me"?* *Don't you know anything? Haven't you been listening?* *God doesn't come and go. God lasts. He's Creator of all you see* [your present] *or imagine* [your potential]. *He doesn't get tired out, doesn't pause to catch his breath. And he knows everything, inside and out.*
> Isaiah 40:27–28 MSG

Life brings opportunities and challenges of all kinds; some we can control and others we can't. We must learn to look for the light found in Jesus. He laid His life down on a cross so we could see and believe. Peace and joy are found in Him. Our Abba, our Father in heaven, will always be there to love us and point us to the light at the cross. He will never give up or forsake us, because He has already been there. We can trust that He knows the way.

20/20 Vision

Proverbs reads, "If people can't see what God is doing, they stumble all over themselves; but when they attend to what he reveals, they are most blessed" (29:18 MSG).

What God, our Father, wants to give us is true 20/20 vision. Perfect vision is the capacity to see with the eyes of both our head and our heart. We will never find our "Greater Yes!" until we find vision—spiritual eyesight that sees beyond our circumstances or conditions and is not restricted by our personal limitations. Spiritual eyesight gives us spiritual insight. It gives us the ability to see and live in another dimension of faith and trust.

If you had unlimited resources and complete freedom to fail, what would you attempt for God? What would you attempt for your family, your marriage, or yourself? Why is it that most people will never see God do extraordinary things in their lives? It is not because God is unwilling or unable. It is the lack of clear vision and unbelief.

As I have reflected on God's vision for me, I now realize that if I can't see it, I will not believe it, and if I can't believe it, I will never live it. I will become stuck, immobilized, and robbed of what God already knows and sees—my potential and destiny.

We will never believe until we are able to see beyond our current perspective. I don't mean the ability to see with our physical eyes or with our mind's eye. It is neither physical nor mental, but spiritual. It is the capacity to see with the eyes of the Spirit, through the eyes of our heart. You could say, "Where your heart is, that's where your vision is."

What I see + What I believe = What I will do

Besides our own vision, there is God's vision. *God's* vision sees us as we can be and as we will become. God sees us as completed masterpieces in Christ Jesus. *Our* visions for our lives will come into perfection when we have the spiritual eyesight to see what God sees. God's sight is not limited; it is always perfect. It involves both the seen and the unseen. The only thing that can limit God's vision for us is our own unbelief. Seeing with faith demands we see with the eyes of our heart. It reminds me of the praise song, "Open the Eyes of My Heart."

Without vision, we do not know what to say "yes" to or what to say "no" to—just like my friend from Chapter 4. What a difference spiritual vision would have made to him!

God wants to reveal your lesser yeses and your "Greater Yes!" It will help you determine what to give your life to and what to leave behind.

Life Is a Riddle

Paul wrote,

> We don't yet see things clearly. We're squinting in a fog, peering through a mist. But it won't be long before the weather clears and the sun [Son] shines bright! We'll see it all then, see it all as clearly as God sees us [our potential and destiny], knowing him directly just as he knows us.
>
> 1 Corinthians 13:12 MSG

When I see myself in a mirror, with the eyes in my head, I do not see what God sees. It is but a "poor reflection" or a "riddle." Compared to what will be revealed, life can be but a riddle and a poor reflection of what we can become in Christ Jesus.

Have you ever tried to solve a riddle on your own? Without clear spiritual insight, we look at life through a series of mirrors. Life then looks like a chain of stressful changes instead of a succession of strategic choices. And we wonder why so many are stumbling around in the dark. Life without divine insight, 20/20 vision, is but a riddle.

A Matter of Perspective

Perspective defines what we see and why we see the way do. We often say, "From my perspective, this is how I see it." Why do we see circumstances and people the way we do?

There are two perspectives we have to consider:

Our Perspective	God's Perspective
Fuzzy/Riddle	Clear/Focused
Limited potential	Unlimited potential
Based on fact	Based on faith
Limited by our capacity and condition	Limited only by our unbelief
Blinds us to our destiny	Propels us to our destiny

We might say, "I saw the sun rise today." That is a normal observation. From our perspective, that's what we see. But just because everyone in the world may say something, that doesn't necessarily make it true. Technically, the sun does not rise or set—the earth, revolving on its axis, makes the sun *appear* to "rise." Of course, several hundred years ago, when people believed the sun actually revolved around the earth, a rising and setting sun made sense.

However, we now know the earth is not the center of the universe anymore than we are. The Son (Jesus Christ) is the center of our universe, and we need to see life from His perspective, not ours. "Normal" is what he says, not simply what we feel or believe. If you cannot see from God's perspective, life will always be a riddle.

A few years ago, my son Doug and I had a discussion about what is normal. From the world's perspective, whatever everyone is doing or believing is classified as "normal." But that's not what God says. The world, our culture, wants to persuade you that its perspective is normal, but in reality, living by the world's viewpoint leads to an abnormal life. Normality is set by God, not the media. We have to develop the eyes to see from God's point of view. Then we can actually begin to look at people, places, things, careers, and life situations as God sees them.

When I was in seminary, I sold farm equipment to make a living. At the first farm I had ever visited, I said to the farmer, "Those are the biggest chickens I've ever seen."

"How long have you been doing this?" he asked me.

"Not too long," I admitted.

"Well, son, those are turkeys, not chickens," he informed me. He had to give me a new perspective because mine was pretty fuzzy.

Fortunately, when God sees us, and what we will become, he looks through the grid of Christ, and he sees us complete. Christ in us filters out all our sin, and God sees us as pure and holy, made in his image. God says, *This is my Son, whom I love; with him I am well pleased* (Ma 3:17), because He sees us in Christ. He sees us, as we will become.

Finding My Vision

Isaiah continues: *Yet those who wait for the LORD will gain new strength; they will mount up with wings like eagles, they will run and not get tired, they will walk and not become weary* (Is 40:31 NASB).

What do we have to do to find God's vision for our lives and our "Greater Yes!"?

- *Wait for God.* We will never have the power to rise up to our destiny until we learn to wait on God. Waiting requires that we engage our hearts with God's will, from which our vision must flow.
- *Allow God to mount you up.* God wants to exchange our weak and natural strength for His powerful and supernatural strength.

He wants to exchange our vision, limited by our capacity and condition, for His vision, which is limitless and beyond our comprehension.

- *Get high enough to soar.* Eagles have to get high before they can soar. In the wind currents, they find the power to soar. We need to get our heads up and our knees down, not our knees up and our heads down.
- *Ask God for great vision.* Great vision demands great faith. Great vision is developed from:
  - **A proper view of God's sovereignty**. We have to know who is in control. It doesn't matter what the score is—God wins.
  - **A proper view of God's understanding**. His understanding is far beyond ours. It's inscrutable.
  - **A proper view of God's power**. The power doesn't come from us. The capacity to be the person you need to be will come from God.
  - **A proper view of our need**. We need God. Every morning when I get up, I do two things. I go to my wife and tell her I'm sorry for the dumb things I will do, and I go to God and pray, "God, lift me up. Let me see life from Your viewpoint. I don't want to live life from my perspective, but Yours. I want to see what I can become."

When Michelangelo was commissioned to create the statue of David, he searched extensively until he found a perfect piece of granite. After putting the marble in place, he spent months studying the piece until he could see the completed image in his own mind's eye. The creation came to life as he simply began to chip away what did not conform to his mental image. That's what God does in our life: He chips away what does not belong there.

Without vision, our lives are but a piece of marble, a riddle. When we learn to see what God sees, we will gain the vision for what we can become, our "Greater Yes!" If we never see it, we will not believe it, and we will never reach our God-given potential and destiny. God wants to chip away what does not belong there. Are you ready?

Imagine the possibilities!

MOVING TOWARD MY "GREATER YES!"

1. What do I see when I encounter people on a daily basis?

2. What do I feel when I encounter people on a daily basis?

3. What am I doing to meet the unmet needs of people I encounter on a daily basis?

4. What breaks my heart, and what do I lose sleep over?

5. What have I learned that will help me move to my "Greater Yes!"?

MY PRAYER OF COMMITMENT

Father, I desire to do something great for You! I am committed to succeed at the things that really matter. I am willing to say no to ____(Example: My resentment)____ *because I have a "Greater Yes!" I seek to enthusiastically serve You and others. I know I need to break out of my* ___(Example: Past)___ *and rise to new heights. I ask You to give me a heart that breaks over the people and things that break Your heart. I know I can live my life in such a way that it echoes in eternity. I pray this prayer for Your glory and Yours alone. Amen.*

CHAPTER 9

A Critical Call

What is God laying on your heart that could only have come from Him?

Shortly after I graduated from high school, I was lying on my bunk bed, pondering my future. Although I had worked diligently in academics and sports to earn enough scholarships to completely fund my college education, I had a sense that God was calling me to a greater destiny. However, I had determined in my mind that I was never going into the ministry. (By the way, never tell God "never." You become a big target!)

As I was lying there, my mom came into my room and said, "I want to pray for you. I know you're struggling. All your life I've known God's call was on you and also I know you've been fighting it for years. But I want you to consider what God is saying to you."

That was not what I wanted to hear! I'd been a good Christian, and I had gone to church, Sunday school, and youth group. I even carried my Bible to school. I was a class president, and I tried to be a good representative for Christ. That was enough, right?

I wrestled with her words for a few more weeks, but finally made a choice to follow God's dream for my life. I made the decision to go to Bible college and learn to preach the good news to the poor, open blind spiritual eyes, heal the broken-hearted, and set the captives free (Is 61:1). After thirty-five years, I'm still doing it.

Each of us has been called. There is no exception. You might be thinking, "Well, you don't know where I've been and what I've done to myself and others." "You don't know what I'm going through or dealing with." I don't need to know. The fact is that God has a call on your life. It's not a matter of *if*. It's *when*. The call went out two thousand years ago. Christ died on the cross, resurrected, and made a way for every believer to experience his or her potential and destiny. When are you going to respond to His call?

Paul confirms in his writings:

> God knew what he was doing from the very beginning. He decided from the outset to shape the lives of those who love him along the same lines as the life of his Son. The Son stands first in the line of humanity he restored. We see the original and intended shape of our lives there in him. After God made that decision of what his children should be like, he followed it up by calling people by name. After he called them by name, he set them on a solid basis with himself. And then, after getting them established, he stayed with them to the end, gloriously completing what he had begun.
>
> Romans 8:29–30 MSG

God is calling each of us by name. He calls us first to become one of His children and then calls us to a "Greater Yes!" He knows exactly who you are, exactly what you're going through, exactly where you came from—and He really wants you!

I once heard a woman lament, "God can't use me because I'm divorced." I asked her, "Who told you that lie?"

She was taken aback, but she began, "Well, everybody knows when you're divorced…"

"That's a lie," I interrupted her. "Your condition, your past, pain, or shame does not determine your destiny." The woman began to cry. She had been divorced for twenty-five years, and she had believed that lie the whole time. You ought to see what she is doing for God now! She has developed an incredible ministry to single mothers and the poor.

God is calling you just as you are, with all your "stuff." He doesn't say, "Get cleaned up and change into a perfect person, someone I can use." Instead, he is calling you in your imperfection, "I'll use you just the way you are. In fact, I'll use what you've gone through to propel you to your potential." First, you must answer the call, and then He will cleanse you, restore you, complete you, and transform you.

Paul assured us that whatever God has promised gets stamped with the "Yes of Jesus" (2 Co 1:20 MSG). God's yes and our yes together become our "Greater Yes!"

Isn't that great? When our yes combines with Christ's yes, something new and incredible is born. God wants to meet the desires of your heart and fulfill you. To do that, He puts Christ's Yes within you, stamped with the Spirit's guarantee that He will complete what He started. He calls the unqualified and qualifies the called. God is calling us to become more than we can become on our own. Every person has a call of God on his or her life. How we express it is limitless!

God's Call + Your Obedience + God's Provision = Your "Greater Yes!"

God in the Flesh

Years ago I accepted a call to a church outside of Chicago. My daughter was in junior high, and I knew she was struggling with the move. When I asked her how she was doing, she said, "Not so good. I just wish I had one close friend."

"God will be your friend," I responded.

She looked at me rather sternly and said, "It is hard going to the mall with God." It took me awhile to realize that she really did need a friend who would be "like God in the flesh."

We are to be a representative of God in the flesh. Just as Christ came to reconcile all mankind to the Father, there is a general call to all believers that Paul clearly lays out:

> *Therefore, if anyone is in Christ, he is a new creation; the old has gone, the new has come! All this is from God, who reconciled us to himself through Christ and gave us the **ministry** of reconciliation; that God was reconciling the world to himself in Christ, not counting men's sins against them. And he has committed to us the **message** of reconciliation. We are therefore Christ's ambassadors [**mission**], as though God were making his appeal through us. We implore you on Christ's behalf: Be reconciled to God [**model**]"* (author's emphases).

2 Corinthians 5:17–20

Now, since we've been reconciled, it is our responsibility to help reconcile *others* to God. That's what we've been called to do. *How* we do that is our "Greater Yes!"—our means to the end. But the end does not change. Our critical call always challenges us to be reconciled to God and each other, and to help reconcile others to God. Our general call can be quite specific.

We are called to:

• Be a model of reconciliation (2 Co 5:17, 20b)

- A ministry of reconciliation (v. 18)
- A message of reconciliation (v. 19)
- A mission of reconciliation (v. 20a)

Distinctives of Our Critical Call

It is initiated by God. Our critical call is not based on what we can do—it's based on what He has already done. It's His pledge, His promise, to do something powerful in us and through us.

It requires that we see what God sees. You have to develop the eyes of your heart. If we only look through our own eyes, we see the condition—the pain, the sin, the addiction. God sees the unmet needs, the potential, and the destiny.

It is not conditional. Our critical call is given to us on the basis of grace. It doesn't matter if you've been divorced, how many times you've sinned, or how long you've been a Christian—God does not put a condition on your calling.

It is irrevocable. God won't take the call away. Paul wrote: *For God's gifts and his call are irrevocable* (Ro 11:29). *The Message* paraphrases the verse: *God's gifts and God's call are under warranty—never canceled, never rescinded*. God's gifts are based on His faithfulness, not your condition.

It moves us toward our destiny. Because it's based on God's power, our call always moves us *toward*, not *from* our destiny. We concentrate so hard on trying to break free *from* something, when all along God is saying, "Forgive your past. I'm going to break you free *to* your 'Greater Yes!' and *to* your calling."

It is eternal. God made a pledge with you by giving the Holy Spirit, sealing your destiny in Christ. Apart from Christ you can do nothing, but in Him you are complete, finished.

It leads us into worship. Jonah kept running away from God's call, but God's call kept chasing him down. When Jonah finally accepted his call, he worshiped God (Jon 2). Our call will lead us to worship in the very presence of God.

It involves meeting unmet needs. God is calling us to do his work: meeting the unmet needs of people. That's what my dad did for thirty-eight years while he ministered to the Native Americans. People asked, "How can you live in that situation, with no running water and outhouses?" But my dad didn't see the conditions on the reservation. Instead, he looked through God's eyes and saw only people in need of Jesus.

It is by choice, not by chance. When I got up this morning I made a choice to spend an hour with God. I'm not a saint, but I have realized I am living my potential by the choices I make. What is your potential? What are you choosing? It doesn't matter how old or young, rich or poor you are—you can choose God's destiny for you. He is calling you!

How Do We Hear Our Critical Call?

Elijah answered this question.

> *Then a great and powerful wind tore the mountains apart and shattered the rocks before the LORD, but the LORD was not in the wind. After the wind there was an earthquake, but the LORD was not in the earthquake. After the earthquake came a fire, but the LORD was not in the fire. And after the fire came a gentle whisper. When Elijah heard it, he pulled his cloak over his face and went out and stood at the mouth of the cave. Then a voice said to him...*
>
> 1 Kings 19:11-14

God's voice wasn't in the wind, the earthquake, or the fire—all extremely loud voices. All kinds of fads and gimmicks attempt to get our attention, maybe even shake up our lives, but that's not where we find God's voice.

Elijah found out that God's voice was the gentle and quiet whisper. Sadly, we let our lives get so noisy sometimes that we can't hear the still, small voice. The desperation of the voice you hear may give you a hint whether it is the world's cause or God's calling to which you are listening.

Our Critical Call Leads Us to Our "Greater Yes!"

Scripture holds countless examples of men and women who answered God's call and discovered their "Greater Yes!"

- As the first man, Adam was called to multiply and subdue the earth.
- Noah was called to build a boat when it had never rained.
- Abraham was called from idolatry to be a father of many nations.
- Jonah was called out of a fish to preach to a people he despised.
- Joseph was called out of a pit to provide for Israel's future.
- Moses was called to stand before a Pharaoh who would not let God's people go.

- Joshua was called to lead Israel into a Promised Land infested with giants.
- Daniel was called to speak for God when no one wanted to listen.
- David was called out of his sin to be a man after God's own heart.
- Mary was called to give birth to the King without the advantage of marriage.
- Peter was called to leave his successful business to become a fisher of men.
- A little boy was called to give his lunch so God could perform a miracle.
- Mary Magdalene was called out of her past to anoint Christ for burial.
- Lazarus was called from death to live again.
- Jesus was called from heaven to reconcile all mankind to God, the Father.

God has called all of us. The only thing that can hold us back is the choice we need to make to respond to the call. Rise up to follow your destiny!

If not now, when?
If not here, where?
If not you, who?

Imagine the possibilities!

MOVING TOWARD MY "GREATER YES!"

1. What is God laying on my heart that could only have come from Him?

2. What is God calling me from?

3. What is God calling me to that causes my heart to break?

4. What is standing between me and God's call in my life?

5. What have I learned that will help me move toward my "Greater Yes!"?

MY PRAYER OF COMMITMENT

God, I know You have called me to something greater. Help me to hear the still, small voice and follow Your call for my life. I want to get rid of anything standing in the way and keeping me from my "Greater Yes!" Amen.

➥ CHAPTER 10 ➥

Engaging Your God-Given
Passions and Desires

*What has God put in your heart that causes
your heart to break?*

During my freshman year of college I met the love of my life, Cathy. After only one date I knew she was the one, and I asked her to marry me. What is so amazing to me even now is that she felt the same way and said, "Yes!" Even though I did not know her well, I fell passionately in love with her, and I wanted her to be the "Yes!" of my life. That was more than thirty-five years ago.

Before we were engaged, I had made a commitment that I would spend the summer on the reservation helping my dad build a church. It was hard, hot work, and I missed Cathy incredibly, but God and His call had to come first.

I lived on the reservation for more than two months that summer, and every day Cathy wrote to me. Her letters expressed her passion and love for me. I was lonely, but the letters seemed to bring us closer together. Every other week her dad allowed me to call collect. The one phone booth on the whole reservation was full of bugs, but I would talk to her as long as the bugs would allow. I was so in love. I battled flying insects from my eyes, mouth, and down my shirt while little creatures crawled up my pant legs. All in the name of passion!

If we are going to pursue our "Greater Yes!", it will require engaging our God-given passion and desires. It is what motivates us to keep going when there is more month than paycheck, when the pipes freeze, the kids are sick, the car breaks down again, and it seems that not even God cares.

Passion can be defined as an inner force, power, zeal, or enthusiasm for something or someone. It moves, motivates, stirs, drives, compels, and propels us to our potential and destiny.

The real question we must ask ourselves is: What is God asking us to pursue with all of our heart, soul, mind, and strength? That is the "yes" of our passion and desire. What gets you up in the morning, keeps you up late at night, motivates you to give beyond personal strength, drives you to your knees, and moves you toward your potential and destiny? That is a God-given passion.

Whatever you pursue with all your passion will become the "Yes!" of your life. The Bible says, *For where your treasure is, there your heart [passion] will be also* (Ma 6:21). Where you find your identity and significance will become the passion of your life.

If you are going to engage your God-given passion and desires, you have to, "*Love the Lord your God with all of your heart [passion] and with all your soul [desire] and with all your mind [understanding]*" and "*Love your neighbor as yourself*" (Ma 22:37–40). This is the conduit for the engaging of our God-given passion and desire.

Love and Passion for God = Our "Greater Yes!"

Our "Greater Yes!" must flow from a deep intimate relationship with God through Jesus Christ. The conduit can only begin when we love God with all of our passion (heart), desire (soul), and understanding (mind). If you want to learn more about how to have this kind of relationship with Jesus Christ, see Chapter 29: First Things First.

Paul understood how critical it was to live a life that expressed his relationship with God through Jesus Christ. He wrote:

> *But whatever was to my profit I now consider loss for the sake of Christ. What is more, I consider everything a loss compared to the surpassing greatness of knowing Christ Jesus my Lord, for whose sake I have lost all things. I consider them rubbish, that I may gain Christ and be found in him, not having a righteousness of my own that comes from the law, but that which is through faith in Christ—the righteousness that comes from God and is by faith. I want to know Christ and the power of his resurrection and the fellowship of sharing in his sufferings, becoming like him in his death, and so, somehow, to attain to the resurrection from the dead.*
>
> Philippians 3:7–11

Paul had an incredible pedigree, a fine education, an impeccable character, and the zeal to persecute Christians. He kept every aspect of the religious laws and was considered *a Hebrew of Hebrews; in regard to the law, a Pharisee,* but he still did not know God (Ph 3:4–6). He came to understand that all his "little yeses" were the very things that kept him from his "Greater Yes!" which flows from knowing Christ Jesus.

The phrase "to know" speaks here of deep, personal relationship. There are people I know as acquaintances, there are those I consider as friends, and there is my family. Each of these groups I know progressively more intimately. But Paul is speaking about something even more intimate. He is referring to the way a man knows his wife—the kind of knowing that develops between a man and woman who have spent years together in the highs and lows of life. I recently met a couple that had been married sixty-five years, and after so long together, they even acted like each other in many ways.

Paul is making it clear that everything he has accomplished or earned on his own is like "dog dung" in comparison to knowing Jesus intimately. Jesus or dog dung: Which do you choose? Paul knew all the successes and accomplishments in the world could not be exchanged for the passion he found in knowing Jesus Christ. Everything he lived for flowed from the intimacy he felt for his Savior.

Paul understood that if we are going to stay focused and know Jesus intimately, we have to:

- Count all competing agendas (little yeses) as loss.
- Count all personal accomplishments as rubbish.
- Realize that Christ satisfies all personal passions and desires.
- Find personal righteousness only through faith in Christ.
- Find power in and fellowship with Jesus Christ through a lifelong pursuit.

The paradox is that when we're willing to lose all we think we have gained or accomplished, we actually gain true passion, potential, and destiny. When we're willing to let all of it go and say, "My first priority is to pursue God, and my passion in life is to serve and worship Him and to find a deep relationship with Him," then we gain our "Greater Yes!"

Our "Greater Yes!" = Love and Passion for Others

When our "Greater Yes!" pursues our God-given passion and desire, we will love our neighbor with all of our heart, soul, mind, and strength. You cannot say you have passion and love for God and not have passion and love for His people.

- When you begin to know God in an intimate way...
- Your heart will begin to break over the same things that break His heart.
- You will see people as God sees them.
- You will become passionate about the people God is passionate about.
- You will weep over the people God weeps over.
- You will become an expression of God's grace and love.
- You will see where God is moving.

What Steals Our God-Given Passion and Desire?

Thrown Focus. Satan doesn't want you to express your God-given passion and desire. He wants to bring little yeses into your life to throw your focus off. He doesn't care if you have passion as long as it does not pursue an intimate relationship with God through Jesus Christ. He knows that our "Greater Yes!" flows out of knowing and pursuing Christ.

Many of us have a purpose, but it's not God's "Yes!" Our passion is crowded with little yeses that don't really matter. If our passion is not focused, whatever we succeed at will be futile, because it won't count for eternity.

Paul warned: *Watch out for those dogs, those men who do evil, those mutilators of the flesh* (Ph 3:2). Some false teachers in the Philippian church were saying that in order to be spiritual, men had to be circumcised. But Paul was warning us to watch out for people or things that will try to throw our focus off of Jesus.

These people were basically saying that your spiritual passion is up to you. Your condition defines and determines your spirituality. If you read the Bible enough, say enough prayers, pay enough tithes, and listen to enough sermons you will be qualified to be used of God. However, our condition (circumcised or not) does not determine or define the depth of our spirituality.

Paul was warning that well-meaning people or things will steal our passion, our focus, and our "Greater Yes!" What is creeping into your life and threatening to steal your spiritual passion? So many things can distract us—careers, addictions, sexual impurity, worry, pride, selfishness—anything that demands your time and energy can quickly take over your passion. Where your heart is, there is your passion!

King David was one of the greatest, most passionate men in the Old Testament—but he was not immune to robbery of passion. In 2 Samuel 11 we find him wandering around his rooftop when he should have been at war (v.1). He checks out Bathsheba, his neighbor's wife, commits adultery with her, and later has her husband murdered.

What brought David to this place? What robbed him of spiritual passion? In a brief time, David went from being a "man after God's own heart" to an adulterer and murderer. Although David was passionate about God, Satan was able to get David to exchange a mission for a mistress.

What mistresses in our lives are we accepting in exchange for our passion for God? David lost focus from his "Greater Yes!" and was taken out. His fall shows us that it doesn't matter how talented or gifted or rich we are—Satan can take us out. Fortunately, when confronted, David repented and returned to his first love.

Self-centeredness. Paul described self-centered passion—anything that takes our focus off of our personal pursuit of a deeper relationship with God through Jesus Christ and his mission and call for our lives.

Paul explained, *If anyone else thinks he has reasons to put confidence in the flesh, I have more* (Ph 3:4). He lists his credentials: he was an orthodox Jew, so he was religious; he was of the right family; he was educated; he had a position; he was a Pharisee; and he was zealous for the Law.

So, why couldn't Paul put confidence in the flesh? Because those credentials were robbing him of spiritual passion. They were certainly great things—I wish I had a résumé like that. But résumés do not pursue God. Men pursue God.

The people, places, and things the world takes pride in keep distracting us from our focus on and relationship with Christ. Our true passion is to pursue God, and our "Greater Yes!" flows out of that pursuit.

A Lifelong Pursuit

Paul concluded his passionate monologue by saying, *Not that I have already obtained all this, or have already been made perfect*—he hadn't arrived yet—*but I press on to take hold of that for which Christ Jesus took hold of me* (Ph 3:12). *The Message* paraphrases this verse: *I'm not say-*

ing that I have this all together, that I have it made. But I am well on my way reaching out for Christ, who has so wondrously reached out for me.

A passionate love for God and others has to be a lifelong pursuit. If we are going to run a race, we have to practice every day. We have to get up, put on our running shoes, stretch, and run with perseverance. It isn't easy, but the goal we keep in mind makes the effort worthwhile. Loving God is my desire and passion, which is expressed through my "Greater Yes!" to others.

When Cathy and I had been married about twenty years I heard a speaker say, "If you want to know how your marriage is doing, ask your wife." So, feeling pretty confident, I went home and asked Cathy, "How is our marriage?"

She looked at me and said, "What marriage? You have to be here to have a marriage." I did not sense any anger or bitterness; I only felt her sadness. She understood that true passion and deep intimacy flow out of real and right relationship.

I had a rude awakening that day. I had lost focus on what really mattered and exchanged intimacy with my wife and family for lesser yeses. I have spent the last fifteen years renewing and rediscovering that first love. I also realized that my relationship with my wife is in direct proportion to my relationship with God.

Let's start a journey of falling madly in love with Jesus Christ by seeking to know Him intimately—and everything else will fall into place.

Imagine the possibilities!

MOVING TOWARD MY "GREATER YES!"

1. What has God put in my heart that causes it to break?

2. What or who is it that I pursue with all my heart, mind, soul, or strength?

3. What are some of the personal mistresses that throw me off from the mission of my "Greater Yes!"?

4. What engages my desires and passions more than anything?

5. What have I learned that will help me move toward my "Greater Yes!"?

MY PRAYER OF COMMITMENT

God, I admit there are so many things in this world that want to draw me away from You. Show me what in my life is robbing me of my spiritual passion and taking me away from my mission. Instead of falling into those desires, I want to be passionate about the things that matter. Help me to fall madly in love with You, passionately seeking Your will and purpose. Amen.

≈ CHAPTER 11 ≈

Evidenced by What Is Unseen

What is God creating in your mind and spirit that could only have come from Him and be accomplished through Him?

It's easy to walk on water if you know where the rocks are. Unfortunately, we usually don't know where all the rocks are. In fact, all we really know is the Creator who made the rocks and the water.

One summer I helped my dad build his first church on the Indian reservation. He gave me clear instructions on how to dig the trenches for the foundation, carefully drawing out on the ground in chalk the auditorium, restrooms, classrooms and living quarters. And I went to work!

When I got to the auditorium, I thought to myself, "This looks way too small. I think I'll make it a little bigger." So I marched off a few feet and made it wider, figuring what they didn't know wouldn't hurt. Only later did I find out that they ran out of blocks.

It was not until the dedication of the building a year later that I confessed what I had done. My dad had just shared how God had so wonderfully provided the new/used pews we were sitting on from a church in Reno. It was like God had allowed these pews to be made to fit perfectly in the new auditorium. But when the truth was made known, we realized God had allowed the auditorium to perfectly fit the donated pews. God knew what we needed, and He loves to do things unseen.

I learned something about faith through that experience. God longs to call us off our map and onto His compass. He wants to expand our faith borders, because He already knows what He is going to do. If we are going to live our "Greater Yes!" we have to begin to believe what we cannot yet see or have not yet experienced.

Hebrews 11:1 is the best-known verse for defining faith. It says:

Now faith is being sure of what we hope for and certain of what we do not see. Another translation (NASB) says: *the assurance of things hoped for.* There are two things we can learn about faith. First, faith is the assurance of things hoped for. Assurance means there's no question in your mind. It's certain and guaranteed. Second, it's being certain of what we do not see. If we can see it, measure it, do it, touch it, move it, motivate it, and charge it, it's probably not faith.

Assurance + Hope + Unseen = Faith

A lot of Christians will say they walk by faith. They really walk by fact.

As an associate pastor for many years, I thought I walked by faith. Of course, I received a paycheck every two weeks, and with more than two thousand people in our church, I wasn't too worried about whether or not the money would come in. Then God said, "I want you to go in another direction. I am calling you off your map onto My compass." For the last few years, since I left that paid position, Cathy and I have truly been on a faith walk. It's based on what we hope for, but not on something that's visible.

God commands us to walk by faith, yet how many of us have ever really put ourselves in a position to be stretched by faith? I'm not talking about charging something to a credit card and saying, "God will provide the money to pay for that." Have you ever truly put everything out on the limb for God?

The writer of Hebrews continues, *By faith we understand that the universe was formed at God's command, so that what is seen was not made out of what was visible* (11:3). The paradox is that what we see (creation) was made by what we don't see (God). As humans, we have a desire to see the facts; we want to know the consequences before we make the decision. But when we walk by faith, we must be able to see beyond what is visible.

Can you be a Christian and not walk by faith? Of course. You can have a faith in Jesus Christ, you can study and read the Bible and still not *walk* by faith. Many Christians who say, "I believe in Christ; I'm going to heaven," have a set of religious rules they obey, and believe by following them they will have enough of God to go to heaven. What if we had enough of God to walk every day by faith? To trust in the invisible? I believe it would require a deeper, intimate relationship with God.

Questions about Faith

What is the opposite of faith? Things like doubt, unbelief, fear, and self-confidence are always the opposite of faith. They cause us to look to ourselves for help in life instead of looking to God. Another big opposite of faith is worry. Worry is concern out of control. Sometimes instead of having faith that God can and will come through for us, we get worried because we realize our own limitations. Faith counts on our limitations.

How much faith is enough faith? When you sit down in a chair, you don't pick it up first and test the strength of the wood or metal or ask someone else to sit there first. Most of us just plop down and have faith that the chair will hold us up. We don't know who made it, or how it was made, but we have no reason to believe that it won't support us. Everybody has a measure of faith in one thing or another.

How does one increase faith? Why could David face Goliath? Because he had seen God provide in the past. David had killed the lion and the bear, and Goliath was no different because David's faith had grown with the size of his enemy. Our faith is built as we see God come through again and again. Personally, I haven't faced Goliath. I don't get up in the morning and say, "God, build my faith," because I know what that means. Some big Goliath is going to come my way in the form of a person or circumstance in my life. When you start praying, "God, increase my faith," there will be challenges. God allows difficulties in our lives according to our faith.

Satan does not care if we have enough faith to go to heaven. He can't do anything about that. Going to church, paying tithes, and all those things that "good church people do" don't matter to our enemy. But God is trying to make us warriors, and Satan doesn't want warriors. He doesn't want anyone to have the ability to stand up against Goliath. There will always be church, because there will always be good, religious people. However, when you start standing up and saying, "My God is able to do anything great and mighty," Satan is going to come against you.

Job had a wonderful response to Satan's attack. He stayed true to God. He said: *Though he slay me, yet will I hope in him* (Job 13:15). That's a man of faith.

How does one lose faith? I'm not referring to losing our salvation (saving faith). The faith we can lose is the faith to be able to walk and be courageous, to stand up to Satan and say, "You will not have my family. You will not have my life. You will not have my church." God is looking for warriors, people of faith—not just people who have a faith.

I don't know if I can muster up enough faith. I don't know what it takes to see lives changed through my efforts, but I'm going to find out, because I believe that our faith is increased not according to the amount of our faith, but by the focus of our faith.

Faith + Vision = Your "Greater Yes!"

Facts about Faith

Faith is not based on the amount of your faith. The disciples said, *Increase our faith.* Jesus responded, *"If you have faith as small as a mustard seed, you can say to this mulberry tree, 'Be uprooted and planted in the sea,' and it will obey you"* (Lk 17:5–6). The mustard seed is almost microscopic, but it grows into a huge plant.

Even though I don't personally know any of the guys who build airplanes or the pilots who fly them, I fly all the time by faith. I trust my life to people I haven't even met. Because I know God intimately, how much more should I trust him with everything?

You could have the faith of a mustard seed. There isn't anything God can't do through you, if it is according to His plan, and if you have enough faith. I haven't met anybody who didn't at least have the faith of a grain of a mustard seed.

Faith is based on the focus of your faith—it is not blind faith. Although we can't see God, we do have a focus for our faith. It's based on our relationship with God and His faithfulness to us.

When Peter walked on the water, what was the problem? He took his eyes off of Jesus, and he sank. As long as he had his eyes on Jesus, he could walk on water. When I studied theology, one theory I heard was that Peter, as a fisherman, knew where the rocks were, and used them to walk on the water. But I believe he walked by staying focused on Jesus Christ.

Faith is founded on God's Word. Jesus passed by a fig tree. He was hungry, but there was no fruit on the tree, so he cursed it. The next morning the disciples find that the fig tree has withered overnight. Jesus says to them, *"Whatever you ask for in prayer, believe that you have received it, and it will be yours"* (Mk 11:24).

That's a big promise. You mean if I ask for a Mercedes, I will get it?

No, because there's an assumption in this passage. *This is the confidence we have in approaching God: that if we ask anything according to his will, he hears us* (1 Jo 5:14). Many of us are praying and teaching people to pray by faith for things God has no desire for us to have. He is not interested in a name-it-and-claim-it game.

If we've been communing with God and reading His Word, we're going to pray according to His will. And if we pray according to His will, it will be done.

Sometimes I worry-pray. Do you ever worry-pray in the midst of your concern? As he started to sink, Peter cried out to Jesus to save him. I don't know how many times in the midst of crying out to God I've said, "God, I don't have enough faith; increase my faith," and God reaches down and, like Peter, pulls me up.

Faith is conditional to love. Paul wrote: *If I have a faith that can move mountains, but have not love, I am nothing* (1 Co 13:2). Faith is always conditional to love. If we don't love our brothers, what happens to our faith? God doesn't honor it.

Without faith you cannot please God. Hebrews 11:6 lays this out, plain as day: *Without faith it is impossible to please God, because anyone who comes to him must believe that he exists and that he rewards those who earnestly seek him.*

Christians have been confused about the principles of blessing. We often think blessings are material things, so if we have faith, we'll get stuff. But Hebrews 11:6 shows the real heart of faith—earnestly seeking God. The deeper my relationship with God, the more faith I have. The real blessing is not the stuff; it is the relationship. We should know God so well that we wouldn't ask anything not according to his will.

Faith reveals God to you. Without faith, it is impossible to know God. It is tempting to say, "God, please appear in physical form and then I can believe you." God's reply is, "Anybody can live that way. What I want you to do is live by faith, not by sight." That faith will make God real to us.

Faith reveals God's grace, righteousness, and justification for us. In Romans 4:3 Paul reminds us: *What does the Scripture say? "Abraham believed God, and it was credited to him as righteousness."* Later Paul wrote: *Since we have been justified through faith, we have peace with God through our Lord Jesus Christ, through whom we have gained access by faith into this grace in which we now stand* (Ro 5:1–2).

Martin Luther said, "We are justified by faith and faith alone, all righteousness, all peace, all grace, all justification is by faith." When I go to God, I receive righteousness, peace, grace, and justification. So when someone asks, "Are you a righteous man?" I can say, "Yes, by faith I am a righteous man."

Robbers of Faith

Just as real as the facts of faith are the things which steal our faith.

Fear, doubt, and unbelief. The very antithesis of faith is fear—lack of trust in our faithful Heavenly Father. Jesus asked His disciples: *"Why are you so afraid? Do you still have no faith?"* (Mk 4:40).

Jesus said, *"I tell you the truth, if you have faith and do not doubt......it will be done"* (Ma 21:21).

If *unbelief* robs us of faith, then *belief* gives us faith. *"He [Jesus] could not do any miracles there......he was amazed at their lack of faith [belief]."* (Mk 6:4-6)

Have you ever had a miracle done in your life? Every morning now I pray, "God, I need a miracle." A miracle is simply when God shows up in our time of trouble. How many of us, before going into something as routine as a meeting, go to God first and say, "God, I need you to be with me in this meeting. I don't want to go in without you."

Hard hearts, lost focus, and lost love. When Jesus was feeding the four thousand, he said: *"Why are you talking about having no bread? Do you still not see or understand? Are your hearts hardened? Do you have eyes but fail to see, and ears but fail to hear?"* (Mk 8:17-19) Hard hearts lead to hard heads. When I share with people about what I'm doing and how I trust God for our income and all the things we do, hard-hearted people say, "That's the craziest thing in the world. Are you nuttier than a fruitcake?" Walking by faith and not by sight is totally illogical by the cultural norm. However, our norm should not come from what man says but what God says. Faith is not always logical or practical. An old song I used to sing tells us to "Have faith in God for he is the answer." Lost focus will steal our faith if we let our eyes wander and begin to focus on the circumstance, on the storm, instead of on Jesus. Where your focus is, there your faith will be also.

Our faith is sustained by our passionate love for God and for others. If we lose that, it will rob us of our faith. The "love chapter," 1 Corinthians 13, concludes that, *These three remain: faith, hope and love. But the greatest of these is love* (v. 13). When we get to heaven, our hope will be fulfilled and we will no longer need faith, because we will have sight, but we will still have love.

Faith + Works = Your "Greater Yes!"

James tells us that faith without works is dead (2:14). The "Greater Yes!" is about putting our faith to work.

Do we live by works? No. Are we saved by works? No. We are justified by faith alone. But if you are a man or woman of faith, you will have works. Jesus once cursed a fig tree because it looked like it should have fruit but only had leaves. You may have a lot of leaves, but how is your fruit? A lot of us have Christian activities, and we're busy for Jesus, but we aren't producing any real fruit. Real fruit, like real faith, results in changed lives.

Let Go and Let God! I hate roller coasters! When my two kids were teenagers, they would attempt to get me on a roller coaster for the sheer pleasure of watching me suffer. They would arrange for me to sit right in front of them. They loved to see the panic in my eyes and watch my body language, which cried out with fear while preparing for the worst.

When I got in the roller coaster car, I put my hat under my arm and glasses in my pocket, feet solid on the floor and hands tightly grasping the guardrail. While the car went swiftly down the track, I hung on for dear life, all the while waiting for the car to go off the track. I was determined to keep my body in the car and the car on the track, hating every minute.

Meanwhile my kids were behind me with their hands raised, screaming their lungs out and enjoying every minute. They got a kick out of watching me suffer.

When the ride finally ended the kids were always ready to go again, but I felt beat up and eager to find a safe place just to sit. My fear started with a wrong belief system. Because I did not know the designers and builders of the ride, I couldn't believe it wouldn't go off the track, so I lived in fear and unbelief.

On the other hand, my kids ride by faith. They let go and enjoy the journey. They enjoy the ride within the parameters set by the creator. Life is like that roller coaster with its ups and down, switches and turns. Let go!

Imagine the possibilities!

MOVING TOWARD MY "GREATER YES!"

1. What is God creating in my mind and spirit that could only have come from Him and can only be accomplished through Him?

2. What keeps me from moving off my map?

3. What is robbing my faith?

4. If I had the faith, what would I attempt for God?

5. What have I learned that will help me move toward my "Greater Yes!"?

MY PRAYER OF COMMITMENT

Heavenly Father, You have always been faithful to me. Help me to have faith that is more than just enough to get to heaven. I want to have the faith that moves mountains and attempts great things for You, faith that believes in what I cannot see. Amen!

⌒ CHAPTER 12 ⌒

Driven by a God-Size Need

What is God showing you that is breaking God's heart?

If we are going to really live out our passion and our love for Christ and others, we have to begin to see that behind every problem and condition is an unmet need.

For years, I watched my dad demonstrate unconditional love and compassion as he worked with Native Americans. As a youth, I didn't completely understand it—I thought he felt sorry for and had pity on them. Sometimes, I even thought they were taking advantage of his love and generosity. If they could just get off the reservation and get real jobs, they wouldn't have so many problems.

After years of observing my dad, I realized the problem was mine, not his. I didn't see what he saw. I didn't feel what he felt, and I didn't do what he did. I had pity for people, I felt sorry for people, but I didn't really have compassion for them because I did not want to see or enter into their pain. Pity says, "I am better than you, and I feel sorry for you, because if you were like me, you wouldn't be in that situation."

Behind every condition and problem is an unmet need. My dad saw the unmet need among the Native Americans, and he became God in the flesh. When they were hungry or thirsty, he found food or drink for them. When they needed a friend, he befriended them. (I don't think my dad ever met a man he did not try to like.) When they needed shelter, he took them in. When they were sad, he wept with them, and then he made them laugh. When they were sick or in prison, he visited them, and even when we were cold, he made sure they were warm.

81

Remember the feeding of the five thousand in the Gospel of Mark:

> *When **Jesus** landed and **saw** a large crowd, he had [**felt**] compassion on them, because they were like sheep without a shepherd. So he **began** teaching them many things. By this time it was late in the day, so his **disciples** came to him. "This is a remote place," [**saw**] they said, "and it's already very late. [**felt**] Send the people away so they can go to the surrounding countryside and villages and buy themselves something to eat." [**response**] But he answered, "You give them something to eat."*
>
> Mark 6:34–37 (author's emphases)

The principle from this passage is:

What you see + What you feel + Your response = Your "Greater Yes!"

There is an obvious contract between Christ and the disciples. If we are ever going to develop our "Greater Yes!", we have to develop eyes that see what Jesus sees, a heart that feels what he feels, and faith to respond the way he would respond. The apostle John realized Jesus was testing them, for Jesus already knew what He was going to do (Jo 6:6).

See What Jesus Sees

When Jesus Christ looked at the people, he saw them with the eyes of His Father—He saw sheep without a shepherd. We need to develop the eyes of God in order to see people with compassion the way He does. Christ saw with the eyes of His heart, which were developed by spending time with His Father. He saw the unmet need.

When you pass a homeless person on the street, or notice a beggar while you're shopping downtown, what do you see? Do you pity them and think, "Well, if they just got their act together, they wouldn't be in that situation." Or do you have the heart to see what God sees and feel a desire to reach out to them?

Instead of looking through the eyes of our head, we need to look through the eyes of our heart to develop true compassion for others. What you see will determine how you act. The disciples didn't see people—they saw a desolate place and an inconvenience, so their reaction was to say, "Let's send them away. Let them take care of their own needs."

Our church was holding an outreach to single moms one day, and we were repairing, cleaning, and washing their cars. Several moms were gathered around smoking, and I heard one mom say, "I hope they clean out my car because that's where I live." Many won't say it but they think, "If you would just clean up your life, you would be better off. Just do what the Bible says, and you'll get your life straightened out. Then you wouldn't be living in your car."

Thankfully, God moved my wife to take time to talk with those moms. We found out they had been rejected by other churches. "They don't want us; we're a liability," one single mom said. Through God's eyes we saw women who were hurting, who had been brushed off, cast aside, and were struggling to get by.

The disciples did not even see the people, only the conditions surrounding the people. When we stop focusing on the problems, conditions or circumstances of others, we can see and meet their unmet need.

Feel What Jesus Feels

Jesus saw the needs of the multitudes and felt compassion for them. If we really want to be passionate about Jesus Christ, we need to have compassion for those in need. The dictionary says that to have compassion is to suffer with another or to touch another. In the New Testament it also means to enter into another's pain. In both stories of Jesus feeding the multitude, the Bible says that Jesus saw their need and felt compassion for them.

It is important for us to realize that compassion is not the same thing as pity. You can feel sorry for someone and still have no real desire to participate in her suffering or pain. Pity is always driven by pride; compassion is clothed in humility.

Jesus felt compassion on the hungry multitude because He had been able to see past their circumstance into their unmet need. He entered into their pain. He didn't say, "Well, they're adults, they should be able to take care of themselves." Instead, He saw them as sheep without a shepherd, people in need of salvation.

Because our tendency is to blame people for their own misfortune, we think things like, "If that guy would just quit drinking so much, I'm sure his problems would be solved." We need to look beyond the problem and the circumstance to see the real heart issue. Why is that man an alcoholic? What underlying reasons have brought him to this point?

Can you imagine how our hearts would change if we would say, "God, give me the heart to feel what you feel for people." We would probably be weeping all the time. It would be enough just to catch a glimpse of the way God feels for His lost sheep.

The disciples said, "It's too late to come up with food for them—just send them away." The average church in America is doing the same thing. We want normal people in our church, so we turn a cold shoulder to anyone who doesn't look, act, and dress like we do. But the truth is: it is never too late to feel the compassion Christ feels.

Respond as Jesus Responds

When we have seen what Christ sees and felt what he feels, we will be able to do what he did—actively respond to people's need. He said to the disciples, "You feed them." I've come to the conclusion that it's my responsibility to bring compassion to the world—not my neighbor's responsibility, not Mother Teresa's responsibility, but *my* responsibility. I need to bring the love and compassion of God into the world.

I can guarantee that if you begin to do that, it will change your world. There are days when I don't want to have compassion, and I have to pray, "God, give me the ability, give me the desire to even want to help people, because I've run out of energy." Jesus was weary from speaking to the crowd, but despite His own exhaustion, in the midst of His difficulties, He focused on the needs of others.

I believe God brings opportunities our way to test us. He already knows what he's going to do, but he wants to use us. The little boy who brought his lunch that day was available. He brought his five loaves and two fish to Jesus and said, "Here it is. It's not much, but I'll give it to you." And Jesus was able to do a miracle.

When you see what God sees and feel what He feels, you will begin to seize incredible opportunities. When we bring a blessing to another individual, it blesses us in return—we reap the benefit. The great miracle wasn't that five thousand people were fed. Jesus could have just created some food for the people. But the real miracle was that a little boy gave up his lunch and trusted Jesus for the results. When we become men and women of compassion, we can go out into the world and make a difference—that's the miracle of changed lives.

Seize the Opportunity

The Gospel of Matthew provides in the words of Jesus an amazing description of how we will be judged when time as we know it ends and eternity begins. This passage has troubled me over the years as I wonder what it will be like to stand before God and give an account of the way I've lived my life on earth.

> *When the Son of Man comes in his glory, and all the angels with him, he will sit on his throne in heavenly glory. All the nations will be gathered before him…he will put the sheep on his right and the goats on his left. Then the King will say to those on his right, "Come, you who are blessed by my Father; take your inheritance, the kingdom prepared for you since the creation of the world. For I was hungry and you gave me something to eat, I was thirsty and you gave me something to drink, I was a stranger and you invited me in, I needed clothes and you clothed me, I was sick and you looked after me, I was in prison and you came to visit me…I tell you the truth, whatever you did for one of the least of these brothers of mine, you did for me."*
>
> Matthew 25:31–36, 40

The assumption here is that if you're a believer, you will do these things. That's a powerful assumption, isn't it? I know a young doctor who is leaving his practice to go to Africa and help the poor. Plenty of people think he's crazy. But when you begin to understand this passage and the whole idea of compassion, you start to make different choices. Developing a heart of true compassion will change your whole life. It will redefine how you invest your time, your talent, your treasure, and your touch.

Honestly, I don't know if my lifestyle demonstrates much compassion. It is a struggle for me, but I want to have compassion because it is the heart of God.

Are you ready to stand before God? What will He say to you? Will He say, "I was hungry, and you fed me; I was naked, and you clothed me; I was in prison, and you visited me"? Remember, whatever we do for His people is what we do for Him. When we meet the needs of others, when we are willing to take the role of a servant and wash feet, we will change our world today and impact our eternity.

As long as Satan can keep the church in America confined to its ivory towers and prevent us from getting out, washing dirty feet, and participating in people's pain, the world will be lost. There will be single moms standing around smoking and saying, "Churches don't want us."

As I talked with those moms that day, I heard their unmet need. In my heart, I felt them saying, "The church doesn't want us, so God must not want us." I looked at them and said, "That is not true. God wants you, God loves you, and God cares about you." But our lives sometimes speak so loud they can't hear our words.

It took forty-five minutes, but we cleaned out the car for the woman who lived in it. There were dirty diapers and all kinds of junk in it. It wasn't our dirt—we hadn't put it there—but we felt compassion for her, and it led us to become an instrument of God's love to her and the other single moms that day. We became like God in the flesh.

People with needs are all around us every day. They are people we pass on the street, our waitresses, our grocery clerks, the people who pump our gas, the people we work with, our neighbors across the street—all silently wishing someone would show them kindness.

When we seize those opportunities, God will allow things to come in our lives according to our need. I have realized that when I focus on meeting the needs of others, my own needs are taken care of. Suddenly they don't seem to matter so much. When I'm fixing cars for single moms or serving soup to hungry homeless people, my own desire for a new house or a new car doesn't seem so important anymore.

If you don't see the opportunities, ask God to give you eyes to see what He sees and a heart to feel what He feels. We have to be intentional about it. God wants us to have compassion on others. He didn't give the responsibility only to relief organizations or social programs or the government—He gave it to us.

The church is called to help those in need. Our "Greater Yes!" will meet unmet needs. "You feed them," God is saying to us. Bring your five loaves and two fish or whatever you have and *be* the miracle. See what you can give away or give up. The results are up to God; we just need to make ourselves available.

Imagine the possibilities!

MOVING TOWARD MY "GREATER YES!"

1. What is God showing me and what am I seeing that breaks God's heart?

2. What do I see when I see people in need?

3. What do I feel when I see people in need?

4. What do I do when I see people in need?

5. What have I learned that will help me move toward my "Greater Yes!"?

MY PRAYER OF COMMITMENT

Heavenly Father, thank You so much for loving us and leaving Your glory to meet our unmet need. You didn't just have pity on us, but You entered into our pain and suffering and sin by dying on a cross for us that we might become the instrument of Your grace and love to a world that needs compassion. Help me see what You see, feel what You feel, and respond the way You responded. Amen!

CHAPTER 13

Empowers Our Availability and Abilities

How has God used you in the past and how does He want to use you now?

When my wife and I were first married, we lived with her father, D.J. I remember watching him every day as he took his lunch to work with him. Yet, each day, he would come home and eat lunch with us. Finally, I asked my wife, "Why does your dad always take his lunch to work and then come home and eat again? Is he really that hungry?"

"No," she replied. "He takes his lunch so he can give it away." My father-in-law worked for the railroad, and he would always run into transients who had stowed away on the train. He would ask a guy if he was hungry, then he would offer his lunch and share Christ with the guy while he ate it. He never met one who wasn't hungry.

D.J. worked at the job for forty-three years, and he hated it the whole time, but he found a "Greater Yes!" by sharing his lunch and his faith. That was what he could do. He died a few years ago, and I think he is probably hanging out in a little corner of heaven called "D.J.'s hobos." We'll never really know the extent of the impact he had on people for eternity until we join him there. D.J. knew the formula for miracles.

Your Ability + Your Availability = Your Lunch

In John 6:1–13, we see a young boy who found a "Greater Yes!" Do you think he woke up that day and said, "I'm going to be in the Bible today." No, he probably woke up that day just like any other day, except that he noticed a large crowd was following someone. So he quickly grabbed some bread and fish for lunch and raced off to see what the commotion was about.

As the day wore on, the boy probably forgot all about his lunch in the excitement of listening to this amazing teacher. But when Jesus Christ needed something, the boy was ready. That day, the young boy's lunch became part of his "Greater Yes!" and Jesus used it to miraculously feed five thousand people.

We all have a lunch—abilities and resources God has given us— that we can use to reach our potential and destiny. We just need to be available for him to use us.

As the story began, Jesus noticed the multitude was hungry, and He felt compassion for them, because He saw sheep without a shepherd. So He asked one of His disciples, Philip, "Where shall we buy bread for these people to eat?" (Jo 6:5). In a sense Jesus was saying, "How are we going to meet the unmet needs of these people?" Jesus already knew what He was going to do, but He was testing the disciples to see how they viewed the situation.

Jesus saw the people's condition with compassion—He entered into their pain. The disciples, on the other hand, looked only at their own resources and said, "We don't have enough money to buy bread for all these people."

I know I can't change a life by myself. There are no miracles in me—but there are miracles in the God who is in me. My wife and I made a commitment to walk by faith when we started People Matter Ministries. Although we had only raised about forty percent of our support, we went full time, and we have seen the rest of the money we need come in miraculous ways. We didn't have the resources on our own, but God has provided for us.

The problem is not God or His resources—the problem is our vision and faith. We have to see it before we can believe it. Can we believe God is great enough to do extraordinary things even when it looks like a hopeless cause?

Your Vision + Your Faith = Resources for Your "Greater Yes!"

The disciples searched the crowd and found that little boy with his lunch. He was willing to give it up and trust Jesus for the results, even when he could have said, "What good is my little lunch for so many people? I might as well just keep it for myself and enjoy it."

We ask God the same thing. "God, what good are my abilities and resources when there's a huge world in need?"

God says, "That's not your problem. It's my problem to do the miracles. It's your opportunity to give your lunch."

What's in Your Lunch?

Four key things make up our lunch: our time, our talents, our treasure, and our touch.[1] No one can say, "I don't have anything." We all have our most valuable resource—our time. We have gifts and talents and money that God is asking us to give to him. Are you willing to invest in God? Do you trust that He can take your limited resources and do miraculous things with them? My dad used to say, "I can't take it with me, but I can send it ahead."

Our touch is the ability to love and care for people. God wants your life to touch another life. Even your pain, even your past, even your sin and addiction, God wants to use to propel you to your potential. You need to understand a few things about your lunch:

It originates from the heart of God the Father. As you spend time on your knees before God, he begins to plant in you the seeds of destiny, which will continue to grow, showing you the unmet needs that can be met with your lunch.

It seeks to meet a God-size need. The disciples asked, "What is this among so many?" That's exactly where God wants us—to be in a situation so impossible that it drives us to our knees. Most of us live around the trunk instead of out on a limb. We feel secure on our map, when we know where the lines are, and where we are going. God says, "When are you going to get off your map and move into My compass, where you walk by faith?" There is a God-size need out there and no matter how small your lunch, God can use it to do miracles.

It is not conditional to you. We are full of excuses. "If I could just get rid of this sin in my life," or "If I just had enough money in the bank," or "If I had more creativity." The potential impact of our lunch is not conditional to our circumstance! God loves "Do-Overs." In fact, God can't use us if we think it is all about us.

It is moved by what you see and what you feel. Do you feel pity for people or compassion? Pity never demands that you do anything, but compassion requires you to enter into another's pain. Compassion is driven by what you feel and what you see. When you walk out into the world, what you see will determine what you feel. True compassion will lead you to offer up your time, talent, treasure, and touch to meet unmet needs.

You must see through the eyes of your heart, not your head. We need to pray, "God, let me see what you see." If our hearts are hard, we will not see people with compassion as God does. We will be like the disciples and only see the circumstances and limitations—which will immobilize our potential. But when we look at people through the eyes of a soft and open heart, we will see their unmet needs.

It is based on the understanding that behind every problem, every condition, every circumstance, every desolate place, is an unmet need. When we see a single mother with two or three kids, what do we think? "If she would just get her act together, she could get herself out of that situation." Instead, we need to look beyond to see what God sees—the wounds, the despair, the pain of the past, the unmet needs.

It seeks to meet the unmet need, not just fix the problem. We have to keep our focus on the need. Our tendency is to want to fix the problem. "She's a single mom, so if she could just get married, everything in her life would straighten out." That's not true! If we let Him, God can use our lunch to do so much more than that in her life. We need to be like God in the flesh. That might mean watching the single mom's kids or inviting her to an outreach event or helping her clean the house—whatever it takes to show her she is special to God.

The results are not based on our resources, but God's. The little boy with his five loaves and two fish must have had a tremendous amount of childlike faith to give up his lunch when it looked like it wouldn't do any good. He wasn't thinking, "Well, I just happened to have read scripture, and I know you're going to use this lunch to feed five thousand people, and I'm going to be in the Bible." He was probably thinking, "I'm hungry! What about my problem? I can't do anything about all these other people." But he was willing to let Jesus use his lunch, because Jesus could do something amazing with it. **There are always those who have greater resources but who won't give them.** I have always wondered, "God, why couldn't I be rich so I could help more poor people?" God says to Me very clearly, "Then it would become about you, and you wouldn't need to trust Me." God wants to put us in a position where if He doesn't show up, we're in deep trouble—because that is what pushes us out on a limb and causes our faith to grow. We can't keep waiting around for someone with more resources, more time, more talent, and more abilities to step in. God wants to use *our* lunch, because it will glorify Him.

Don't let anyone despise what you have to offer. People will probably say, "What good can you do with so little? What difference does it make if you spend $30 a month to sponsor a poor child in a third world country when there are a billion others who are still starving!" Don't listen to those voices! God will take your lunch and multiply it thousands of times.

A little miracle goes a long way. There were twelve baskets of food left over after everyone was done eating. Instead of having only what he brought, the little boy was able to eat as much as he wanted—and maybe even take the leftovers home! When we offer up our lunch, guess who really gets blessed? We do. Everybody else gets blessed, but we get blessed more. The resources are not the problem—it's the vision. Are we willing to step out in faith and trust God?

My grandfather, when he was in his nineties, lived with my parents for many years outside the reservation, and he used to walk over to a casino and hand out tracts to people as they left. He couldn't say a lot, his eyesight was failing, and he wasn't a very big man, but he used the resources he had to hand out hundreds of tracts. There will probably be a corner of heaven called "Grandpa's Gamblers Anonymous." I have no idea how many people turned their lives around after reading those tracts. It wasn't my grandfather's job to cure them of being gamblers. He simply saw sheep without a shepherd and offered his lunch.

God is willing to do a miracle through your life, whether you are as old as my grandfather or as young as the little boy with the loaves and the fish. We must simply see people through God's eyes and focus on the unmet needs instead of the desolate circumstances around them.

I don't fear failure. I fear succeeding at things that don't matter. It's not about how big our resources are—it's about how big our vision is.

We each have a lunch, and we need to figure out what it is, so we can give it to God to do something miraculous.

Warnings about Your Lunch

The Gospel According to Matthew contains a warning to believers.

It's also like a man going off on an extended trip. He called his servants together and delegated responsibilities. To one he gave five thousand dollars, to another two thousand, to a third one thousand, depending on their abilities. Then he left. Right off, the first servant went to work and doubled his master's investment. The second did the same. But the man with the single thousand dug a hole and carefully buried his master's money.

Matthew 25:14–18 MSG

When the master came back, he found that the first two servants had invested the money and gave him back double, and he rewarded them. When we take our lunch and invest it in changing lives, we will be rewarded in heaven. The third servant, who had buried the money, thought he was doing something good. "You know I took your investment, God, and I took good care of it, and I took care of myself, and I didn't risk it. I just buried it."

The average believer in this country is burying his talent, his abilities, his touch—what God has given him—because he doesn't have enough faith to give it all back. We are living our new life by old principles, old passions, old purposes, and old potential.

The master was furious with the wicked servant. He said: *That's a terrible way to live! It's criminal to live cautiously like that! If you knew I was after the best, why did you do less than the least? The least you could have done would have been to invest the sum with the bankers, where at least I would have gotten a little interest* (vv. 26–27).

In this story there are several warnings about our lunch.

What God has given is not yours. The master entrusted *his* money to the servants, and they were responsible for what they did with it. God gives us our time, talent, treasure, and touch. We may think we earned them, but they are actually not ours.

If you invest what God has given **now, you will reap later.** My dad is completely broke by the world's standards. He spent thirty-eight years as a missionary, and he never had the opportunity to build up any money for retirement. However, he will receive his reward in heaven. We may not see the results of investing our lunch in this lifetime, but we will see it in eternity.

No excuses please. There isn't one God hasn't heard. He's already given us every reason to trust him, so our excuses won't work.

Don't play it safe. The wicked servant thought he was being cautious by burying the money. That's not what God wants. It will be too late when you get to heaven, so go for it now! Why not? Our God is big enough!

Imagine your potential. Write it down, dream about it, talk about it, do whatever it takes to begin to visualize the difference your lunch can make. What if you decided to spend an hour every week witnessing? Our ministry has dedicated twenty-five percent of our income to go directly to helping the poor. It doesn't seem like much yet, but as it continues to grow, I believe we are going to see some amazing results.

Your Lunch + Your Faith = God's Miracles

God really does want to use us. Give him your lunch, and you will find basketfuls left over.

Imagine the possibilities!

MOVING TOWARD MY "GREATER YES!"

1. What makes up my lunch?

2. What do I have that God wants to use?

3. What is keeping me from giving my lunch to God?

4. What miracle does God want to do through me?

5. What have I learned that will help me move toward my "Greater Yes!"?

MY PRAYER OF COMMITMENT

Heavenly Father, I bring my lunch to You and believe You can do a miracle. I want to see You do incredible things. I believe You can do what seems impossible to me right now. Help me to trust You with my limited resources, my time, talents, and touch, because You can do more with them than I could ever dream. Amen.

CHAPTER 14

Echoes in Eternity

What kind of legacy do you want to leave behind that will echo in eternity?

Pretend for a moment that you knew you had only one year to live. How would you change your daily lifestyle? Would you try to repair some relationships or forgive an old friend? Would you go out and spend money like crazy?

Now, imagine that you had only one *day* to live. What would you say to the people you love? What would you want them to say about you?

I've been married to Cathy for thirty-five years, and I have two children and four grandchildren. I'm sure I would be spending some time telling them how much I love them, how proud I am of them, and how they are God's best.

We normally don't live every day as if it might be our last—but it might be. That's why it is so important that we take time now to think about the legacy we want to leave behind. What do we want people to remember us for? We can choose our own legacy.

In John 13, Jesus Christ was thinking about the last moments of His life. He knew He was about to die, and He was spending His time talking with His disciples, His closest friends. But there was something going on behind the scenes. The disciples were stuck on the controversy of which of them would be the greatest in the kingdom. Can you imagine how you would feel if you knew you were about to die and your kids were spending all the time arguing about who would get the inheritance?

Of course, we can't be too hard on the disciples, because they didn't realize their Master was about to die. They thought Christ was going to overthrow Rome and set up a kingdom right there on earth—and each of them wanted to be the Lord's right-hand man.

True Greatness

We have a misunderstanding of what true greatness is in our culture. Someone said to me the other day, "Joe is such a great guy."

"Why is he a great guy?" I asked.

"Well, he built that big company, and he's got a lot of money."

Our society has put value on people based on what they have achieved in their life, whether they are great actors, athletes, successful business figures, or famous politicians. But none of those things are what God considers greatness. God intends for us to live a life that is not simply successful on earth—but successful in making a difference for eternity.

So, as the disciples debated who would be the greatest, Jesus wanted to show them how much He loved them, and also explain to them something about real greatness and what it means to leave a legacy.

Jesus understood the four questions of life. He understood who He was and whose He was—God's Son. He knew His Father loved Him and was pleased with Him. He knew why He was created—not just to die on a cross, but to do the will of His Father, to reconcile man to God. Finally, Jesus understood what He was destined to become. Someday, He would sit at the right hand of His Father.

John 13:1 says: *It was just before the Passover feast. Jesus knew that the time had come for him to leave this world and go to the Father. Having loved his own who were in the world, he now showed them the full extent of his love.*

If you're like me, you would probably spend the last moments of your life showing your family, your friends, your close relatives, and your children or grandkids the full extent of your love. That's what Jesus was doing here.

Jesus knew that the Father had given Him power over all things. He knew where He had come from—God—and He knew where He was going; He knew why God had created Him, and He understood His destiny because He had a "Greater Yes!"

We cannot do what we were created to do until we have a "Greater Yes!" and understand that we were not born just to go to heaven but for a potential and destiny. Then we are empowered to live our lives in such a way that they echo in eternity.

Dirty Feet

In Jesus' time, when you entered a house, a servant would be there to wash your feet, which would be filthy from walking down the dusty streets of the city barefoot or in sandals. However, because the disciples had rented the room to celebrate the Passover, there was no servant, and none of them wanted to be the one to wash everyone's feet. They were too busy debating who was going to be the greatest.

In our sole account of the foot washing, we read, *Jesus knew that the Father had put all things under his power, and that he had come from God and was returning to God; so he got up from the meal, took off his outer clothing, and wrapped a towel around his waist* (Jo 13:3–4).

Jesus did several important things in this scene. First, He got up. He saw the situation, and He rose to the responsibility. Second, He took off His outer clothing, which represented His position, authority, and power. He laid it aside to serve His disciples so He could show them the full extent of His love.

If we want to leave a legacy, we have to be willing to get up and to lay aside our pride in our position, power, or worldly success. The apostle Paul described how he laid aside his prestige as a Pharisee, a Hebrew, a religious zealot, and considered it all worthless compared to knowing Christ (Ph 3).

Become a Love Servant

Then, Jesus took up a towel and wrapped it around His waist. He became like a servant—not just any servant, but a bondservant, one who served out of love for His master even after He had been set free. Finally, He knelt down and washed their feet, an expression of His deep love for them. As He washed their feet, I can imagine tears fell from His eyes as He realized how much He was going to miss them.

Christ was illustrating the kind of people we need to become if we want to see our "Greater Yes!" deployed in our world. My tendency is to find out what God wants me to do, then grab hold of it and do it in my own power and strength—until I realize that I need to lay aside my pride and become a bondservant.

I believe the water basin illustrates the Church—Christians around the world—and the water is the Holy Spirit. It's the Holy Spirit's job to change people, but it's our job, individually, to be the towel. If we're really going to win the world, we're going to win it with a towel and a water basin filled with the Holy Spirit.

Basins + Water + Towels = Cleansed Lives

There are a bunch of towels in the Church that God wants to use in our culture to change destinies, families, and marriages, but many of us are just sitting there with our water basins. We're filled with the Holy Spirit , but we're not going after our destiny. We're not living out our part of the story.

I have all the Holy Spirit in me, but He doesn't always have all of me. There are areas in my life that I still have not given over to the Holy Spirit. Some of us are like Peter, saying, "What? Lord, you can't wash my feet!" We don't want anyone doing something for us when we are not willing to do it for them.

God says to Peter and to us, "I want to wash you up; I want to cleanse you; I want to send you on your destiny. You'll never understand your full potential until you allow me to clean you up."

I would be pretty picky about whose feet I would clean. Sure, I'll wash the president's feet, or some really important person's feet. But what about the terrorists, the prostitutes, the drug addicts, or the alcoholics? We limit our "Greater Yes!" when we look away from those people. God wants us to go out into the gutters, the places where the downtrodden are, and minister to them. Our church billboards and our lives should read: "If you're a single mother, you're welcome here. If you're a drunk, you're welcome here. If you're a prostitute you're welcome here. If you're downcast, you're welcome here." Can you imagine how that could change our society?

The church in America should be a towel. It's not our job to clean others up—the Holy Spirit will take care of that—but we can be the instrument used by the Spirit to set them free.

We miss the point if we think it is just about washing feet. It's about changed lives, going out where the people are and bringing them in. You can preach sermons and worship and read the Bible all day long and never make a difference.

Love Servants + Towels = True Greatness

Finally, Jesus instructed His disciples, *"Now that I, your Lord and Teacher, have washed your feet, you also should wash one another's feet"* (Jo 13:14). Do you want blessing? Do you want true greatness? Start washing feet, start serving people, and become a towel.

You can choose to follow the destiny God has written for you. What do you want people to say about you? More importantly, what do you want God to say about you when you stand before Him someday? I think I want God to say, "Thanks for being part of the Fellowship of the Towel. Thank you for being willing to wash feet."

The Fellowship of the Towel

I invite you to become a member of the Fellowship of the Towel. The membership requires that you choose greatness by becoming a bondservant, a love servant. I believe Jesus says, "Become my bondservant to a world that is looking for hope." Following this example set by Jesus demands that you live life on a downward momentum, making yourself nothing. How many of you would be willing to be nothing? It insists that Christ and others increase while you willingly decrease. It is reserved for those who choose humility and brokenness, being weak and being last.

It is not achieved by self-will or self-achievement but by self-abandonment. Descending is everything the world created it to be. It is demotion, anonymity, and servanthood, decreasing, losing, and dying. Lose it all. Give it all up. Imagine the possibilities. Greatness is not a measure of will, but rather of self-abandonment. The more you are willing to lose, the Bible says, the more you gain. It is not the best path to greatness. It is the only path to greatness.

The culture screams, "That's not right. True greatness is about moving up, about ascending." Our popular, materialistic, commercial culture proclaims that upward mobility only happens to winners, heroes, the successful, the strong, and the proud. It should be admired and pursued at all costs. One must ascend to fame, money, glory, power, comfort, and pleasure. To *choose* any other way means choosing a path reserved for losers, cowards, failures, and the weak and should be avoided at all costs. That's what the world says.

Yet, I'm asking you to do this. I have asked you to consider another way, the way of the towel. The world will be one with the towel and the water basin. John 13 and Philippians 2 state that choosing to go down will require, first, knowing who you are—which speaks to your identity. It requires that you know whose you are—which speaks to your significance. It requires that you know why you were created— which speaks to your purpose. It requires that you know what you are destined to become—which speaks to your potential. It requires unconditional love—which addresses your heart. It requires unapologetic humility—which addresses your attitude. It requires uncompromising courage—which addresses your response, and then it requires unimaginable blessing—which addresses your reward.

In your consideration of being a member of the Fellowship of the Towel, I'd like you to pray this prayer. I pray this almost every day because I want to be a towel. I'm determined to be a towel and a servant.

God, my Father, I receive Your blessing. I thank You that I can find meaning and purpose by following the way of Your Son. I know the path to true greatness and blessing will lead me to humility, brokenness, and weakness, becoming least, and becoming last. Father, I am not capable. I cannot serve out of my own strength and power. Please birth in me Your Son's attitude and heart. Let my response demonstrate Your love, and Jesus' humility and courage. Thank you for using this bondservant to speak good news to the poor, bind up the brokenhearted, and proclaim freedom and forgiveness to the captives. Father, I choose now and forever to take up Your towel. I pray this in Christ's name. Amen.

If you prayed that prayer and really meant it, I challenge you to become a towel. God wants to deploy you into the world to make a difference, but you need to take on the attitude of the towel, being willing to become least and last in order to fulfill your destiny. Someday you will stand before God, and I imagine He will say, "Well done, my good and faithful servant. Enter into my kingdom. You were an incredible towel and the angels will rejoice in heaven because of the choice you made.

Imagine the possibilities!

MOVING TOWARD MY "GREATER YES!"

1. What kind of legacy do I want to leave behind that will echo in eternity?

2. What do I want people to say about me at my funeral?

3. What would my family or close friends say about me now?

4. What kind of life do I want to live that will echo in eternity?

5. What have I learned that will help me move toward my "Greater Yes!"?

MY PRAYER OF COMMITMENT

God, thank You for helping me find my "Greater Yes!" I want to become a towel the Holy Spirit can use as He cleanses people. Please grow in me a desire to reach people and to put my time into doing what really matters, so I can leave a legacy that echoes in eternity. I want to be able to determine what people will say about me by how I live out every day as Your servant. Amen.

SECTION 3

Developing Your "Greater Yes!"

God is more concerned about the journey than the destination! How is God developing your potential and destiny? Seven essential elements in developing your "Greater Yes!" will allow you to rise up and move off your map and onto God's compass. These are some essentials for you to consider.

- God is asking you to trust Him enough to risk it all.

- God is more concerned about what He is doing in you than with or through you.

- God wants to create in you a higher level of dependency.

- God will always exceed your level of expectancy.

- God wants to turn your thoughts and words into power for your potential.

- God allows adversities and difficulties in your life according to your need.

- God wants you plugging into the power already within you.

You can live your life in such a way it
demands an explanation!

☙ CHAPTER 15 ☙

Can't Play It Safe

If anything is worth living for, it is worth dying for.

If we are going to make an impact in this life and in eternity, we have to be willing to take risks. Too many Christians are content to sit back in church on Sundays and then go about their daily lives during the week without attempting anything great for God.

One day my dad and I were at the church we built on the reservation where we ministered, and my dad was witnessing to a rather large Native American. As he shared with the man how much God loved him, the man pulled out his big Bowie knife and started waving it around. I was about ten years old at the time, and I quickly dashed behind a bench to hide. But my dad held his ground.

"I'm going to cut you into a million little pieces," the angry man threatened.

My dad looked calmly up at him and said, "Then every piece will say 'I love you.'"

The man began to weep when he heard those words. He handed the knife to my dad, and that day he came to Christ. My dad had that knife for years.

As a young kid, I was thinking, I don't ever want to do that. I don't want to risk my life and have some guy wave a knife in my face just for talking about God.

What are you willing to risk? How much are you willing to put on the line to do what God calls you to do? Some of your time or your money? A lot of Christians are willing to give God a little token on Sunday morning to pay their hell insurance. They'll read their Bible once in awhile and maybe listen to a good sermon as long as it doesn't go past noon. That's not risk.

Moving Out!

A scene in the Old Testament describes a battle between the Israelites and the Philistines. At a crossroads, Jonathan, Saul's son, said to his armor-bearer: *Come on now, let's go across to these uncircumcised pagans. Maybe God will work for us. There's no rule that says God can only deliver by using a big army. No one can stop God from saving when he sets his mind to it* (1 Sa 14:6 MSG). Maybe! I need more assurance than that.

I actually relate better to the armor-bearer in this story than to Jonathan. My master is saying, "Let's go over to the enemy, and let's take a risk. Maybe God will show up. Without God, what we want to accomplish would be impossible. Are you willing to go with me?" It is better to move out without all the answers and take a risk than do nothing at all.

I'll be honest—if I were the armor-bearer, I might have said, "Could we pray about this awhile? Let's get enough weapons in our arsenal. Why don't we just go wake up a few more soldiers? Do we really have to do this?"

But Jonathan's armor-bearer said, *"Go ahead. Do what you think best. I'm with you all the way"* (v. 7).

That's the kind of guy I want to be when God says, "Are you willing to move out with Me to the other side?" That's where the enemy is, where it's unsafe, where you're going to be attacked. Are you willing to go?

There's no way I'm going to go in the enemy's camp on my own—but I will go with Christ. Risking is saying, "I'm willing to rise up and move out." Jonathan was stepping into a place where God would have to come through or else they were doomed. He created an opportunity for God to bring the victory. Most people never see God do miraculous things because they never put themselves in a position where they need Him to show up.

The greatest opportunities require risk. If you want to live life to the fullest, you must be willing to trust God and risk everything. You might be thinking, "Dan, you're nuts. What do you mean risk everything?" I mean exactly that—risk everything. Be willing to put everything on the line for God. Don't hold back anything.

We all have good intentions. It's easy to say, "I love God with all my heart. I want to do whatever God wants me to do." The problem is that what our mouths are saying is not always what our hearts are feeling. The hard part is being willing to risk it all for the kingdom of God. That's a challenge I face every day, as I recently left my position at my church to pursue a speaking and writing ministry full time because I believe that is what God has called me to do.

What is holding you back? Jonathan and his armor-bearer were in the camp, where it was safe. They had to leave the camp to face the enemy. What camp do you live in? What is it that keeps you from risking?

Maybe you live in the camp of normality, or the camp of compliance, or the camp of mediocrity, or the camp of secure finances—whatever it might be, you need to ask yourself, "What camp do I love to stay in that keeps me from rising up, moving out, and risking?"

You might not be able to answer that question right now, but I challenge you to cry out with sincerity, "God, show me what is keeping me from moving to the call You have on my life." The world has defined security as enough in the bank, a nice job, a nice house on the hill, a car in the garage. In God's eyes, that's not security at all. I'm not saying we have to give up these things, but we need to evaluate if one of those things is keeping us from finding our "Greater Yes!"

Your Risk + Your Courage + Your Faith = Your Potential

The Truth about Risk

It demands faith, courage, and boldness. We must move from the invisible to the visible so the invisible can become visible. Read the Hall of Faith in Hebrews 11. Those men were not perfect—in fact, the Bible is full of stories of their mistakes—but they were listed in God's Hall of Honor. They were rewarded for the faith and courage that allowed them to risk everything for God.

You will be misunderstood. My dad is still accused of being crazy for staying thirty-eight years and faithfully serving the Native Americans. People tell him, "You gave up your retirement to build a church; you gave up everything." But my dad always says, "I gave up nothing." If you take big risks, many people will misunderstand.

It may mean letting go. There is a story about a guy who fell off a cliff and was clinging desperately to a small bush. He calls out, "Can somebody help me?" God answers him, "Let go." He immediately says, "Anybody else up there?" If he had just trusted God and let go of the bush, he would have realized he was only inches from the ground.

We have trouble letting go of what we think is safe. If we would completely surrender to God, I believe we would be amazed at the results.

It can't be about you, and it can't be about now. If you're going to take a risk for God, it can't be about you. Selfish decisions will not make a difference for eternity. When we are only concerned about what will give us happiness right now, we won't be able to have an eternal perspective. What we are willing to risk must be seen in light of eternity.

It may mean walking away. In fact, taking risks may demand that we walk away from a lot of things—the security of a good career or the comfort of a nice house or some of the things we love to do. I am not implying these kinds of things are bad. They may be the very things God wants to use to carry out your "Greater Yes!" God may never ask you to sell your house or quit your job—but would you be willing if it was part of His plan for you? Although it will be different for every person, it will always be worth it, because we will be walking *to* something greater.

When Should We Take a Risk?

There are times when the things we risk aren't really of God. So how do you know if He's calling you to risk something? Here are a few things to check for:

When you have God's peace. I was invited to be an executive pastor of a church in Chicago, so I flew out with Cathy for the interview. However, as we were lying in bed in our hotel room afterwards, she said, "Let's get on the airplane and go home. We'll just give the money back for the plane tickets."

I said, "What? Are you crazy?" (I said it much more lovingly than that.)

"I don't feel right about it," she replied.

"What do feelings have to do with anything?" I asked. So I packed up my whole family and moved them to Chicago. Six months later, I resigned. My wife sensed something that I hadn't—and my whole family paid for my mistake. Although I didn't have the peace of God, I risked my family's happiness because I was tempted by the position.

Was I out of God's will? Maybe, but God never says, "Oops." I think God often says, "Hey, did you learn something? How did that work for you? Now let's try again." Even when we are outside of God's will, His purposes cannot be thwarted. He can use even our disobedience or floundering to teach us something new about His grace and mercy. God can use every right or wrong decision we make and work it out for our good, our potential and destiny (Ro 8:28–30). It is best to make sure you have God's peace and your mate's when you think about taking a risk.

When you know it's not disobedience. A friend came to me once and said, "I'm going to leave my wife. After all, doesn't God want me to be happy?" That's a lot of V.R.G.—Verbalized Religious Garbage. When you know something is disobedient and against God's Word, *don't do it!* Anybody who says, "Oh, God just wants me to be happy," has not read the Word carefully. God wants us to be obedient, and if we're obedient, we'll have His joy.

When you know it will not sidetrack God's will for your life. Since I now have to depend on support to fund my ministry, I often have well-meaning people come to me and give me ideas on how I can raise extra money. They are basically saying, "When God does not show up, I have a backup plan for you." Sometimes I get tempted to try their ideas to build my own financial security. Cathy will come up to me and say, "What are you doing?" She knows me too well. She can tell when I'm getting sidetracked from my calling.

When your spouse is in complete support of the decision. I will never again move an inch without making sure my wife feels right about it. I learned my lesson from our time in Chicago. If you've done your homework and you've prayed and talked to God about the risk you're considering but your spouse does not approve, you need to rein yourself in. Even if you know it's from God, you need to wait until your husband or wife is ready. If you're not married, then ask your parents, pastor, or someone you trust.

When you know it will not hurt or take advantage of someone else. When I decided to take the risk of moving my family to Chicago, I ended up hurting my family in the process. If it's going to hurt someone, it's not from God.

When you know it will further the kingdom of God. If it doesn't, don't risk it. God's kingdom will come whether you take a risk or not, but I want to be part of the process of bringing God's kingdom to earth.

When you know that this decision will bring you more joy in life. God should get all the glory. So if your risk is going to bring *you* the glory, it's the wrong decision. A friend of mine often says, "When we give God all the praise and glory, we get all the joy."

These are not all the conditions—you can probably add some of your own—but they are the ones I've learned from the mistakes I've made.

Is It Worth It?

Paul understood the risk, and he thought it was worth it. He wrote:

> *I feel compelled to go to Jerusalem. I'm completely in the dark about what will happen when I get there. I do know that it won't be any picnic, for the Holy Spirit has let me know repeatedly and clearly that there are hard times and imprisonment ahead.* **But that matters little.** *What matters most to me is to finish what God started: the job the Master Jesus gave me of letting everyone I meet know all about this incredibly extravagant generosity of God.*
>
> Acts 20:22–24 MSG (author's emphasis)

This decision would put it all on the line for Paul. He felt it was worth it for the sake of his "Greater Yes!" Do you feel what Paul felt? Do you hear what God's asking you? Whatever God desires you to do, do it boldly, whatever the cost. Circumstances cannot rob you of the joy of life. And if you will give your life for God's risky business, you will find that you can do all these things through the power of Him who gives you strength.

Imagine the possibilities!

MOVING TOWARD MY "GREATER YES!"

1. What is God asking me to do that only He can do through me?

2. What keeps me from doing the impossible?

3. After listing what I'm afraid to risk losing and what I truly want to gain, how many of them have eternal value in building God's kingdom?

4. What is throwing off the focus of my faith?

5. What have I learned that will help me move toward my "Greater Yes!"?

MY PRAYER OF COMMITMENT

God, I am ready to take a risk for You. Please show me what I need to give up to become the man or woman You will use to accomplish great things for You. Help me to have boldness and courage to take the risks that fuel my "Greater Yes!" Amen.

~ CHAPTER 16 ~

Starts from the Inside Out

God is more concerned about what He is doing in you,
than with or through you.

As parents, we love to hear our children say, "Daddy, when I grow up, I want to be just like you," or "Mommy, when I'm big, I'm going to be like you."

Jesus Christ wants to hear the same thing from us. I believe this principle: No change, no Jesus. If your life is not marked by continual transformation into the likeness of Christ, you are not allowing Him to have complete control of your life. We need to ask ourselves: "Am I more like Christ now than I was ten years ago?"

The world is pressing at us, trying to push us into its mold and make us look like everyone else. However, we were not created to fit in—we were created to stand out!

Conform means to shape into a likeness, and transformation refers to the process of getting there. God uses the process of transformation to conform us into the image of His Son.

The apostle Paul wrote: *Join with others in following my example, brothers.* (Ph 3:17). I used to think that was a pretty egotistical statement to make, but I have realized he was able to say that because he was truly being conformed into the image of Christ. He was saying, "Follow me as I follow Christ." "Imitate me as I mimic Christ."

He continued,

For many walk, of whom I often told you, and now tell you even weeping, that they are enemies of the cross of Christ, whose end is destruction, whose god is their appetite, and whose glory is in their shame, who set their minds on earthly things.

111

> *For our citizenship is in heaven, from which also we eagerly wait for*
> *a Savior, the Lord Jesus Christ; who will **transform** the body of our*
> *humble state into **conformity** with the body of His glory, by the ex-*
> *ertion of the power that He has even to subject all things to Himself.*
> Philippians 3:18–21 NASB (author's emphases)

God is in the process of conforming/transforming us into the image
of His Son, into the image of glory we will be someday. But at the
same time, we are being pulled in another direction by the world's tactics.

Your Conforming + Your Transforming = Christ Image in You!

Conforming to the World

Paul lists several ways that the world attempts to conform us. The first
way is by our appetites. That can be addictions, movies, a way of living, the desire for more stuff—any craving that will suck us into its set
of beliefs. Thousands of advertisements bombard us every day, offering everything from the latest gadget to a $50,000 car to satisfy the ap-
petite the world has created in us.

Second, the world wants us to conform to *its glory*. Paul said the
world's glory is its shame. Our society prides itself on its acceptance of
abortion, gay marriage, divorce, and so many other things that have
undermined God's intention for us. We make athletes into heroes, and
revere the rich and famous. Earthly glory is achieved through wealth,
power, and status—and it seems normal to us. Every day, commercials
scream that we need those things and that we need to conform to the
worldly way of life in order to be happy.

The third thing the world wants us to conform to is *its thinking*.
Some evolutionists may say, "We came from the same ancestors as
monkeys; it just makes sense." The public schools say, "You can't pray
here; that's not fair to everyone." The world's thinking has crept into
every arena of life, pushing us to either conform or face ridicule.

Finally, the world wants us to conform to *its abnormalities*. We have
accepted things that God never intended to be a part of the human
race. Divorce, abortion, and gay marriage are a few of the "hot" issues
right now, but other things that are an accepted part of our society also
grieve the heart of God. 1 John 2:16 (NASB) tells us there are three
ways the world tries to transform us into conformity with it: the lust
of the flesh, the lust of the eyes, and the pride of life. They are the

same three ways that Satan tempted Christ in the wilderness (Ma 4). Even way back in the Garden, Satan tempted Eve with the apple (appetite) and the idea of being like God (glory).

These are not new tactics—our enemy has been using them for thousands of years. But the world has found a way to cause them to creep slowly into our lives so we barely notice. We need to open our eyes!

Being Transformed by God

Developing our "Greater Yes!" will require that we recognize and reject the ways in which the world is trying to conform us, and open our hearts to God's transforming power. The following clearly outlines ways we are conformed to the image of Christ.

> *And we know that in all things God works for the good of those who love him, who have been called according to his purpose. For those God foreknew he also predestined to be conformed to the likeness of his Son, that he might be the firstborn among many brothers. And those he predestined, he also called; those he called, he also justified; those he justified, he also glorified.*
>
> Romans 8:28–30

God didn't create any junk. Every person is a wonderful, incredible creation of God. I have a friend who creates beautiful pottery. He first creates in his mind the image of the finished work. Then he carefully molds the image he sees into the clay and discards what does not belong. God works in our lives in much the same way. He seeks to discard anything in our lives that prevents us from becoming just like Jesus.

Specifically, God wants to conform us to His promise, His purpose, His potential, and His process. God has given us a promise—if you love Him, you're called according to His purpose. Whether you like it or not, He's going to conform you because He loves you too much to keep you the way you are.

A child may be four and still being potty trained, but when he's fourteen, he had better not be wearing diapers. His parents love him too much to let him stay the way he is. Like a sculptor of lives, God loves us too much to keep us as a giant piece of marble. He wants to create us in the image of His Son.

Imagine getting up in the morning and saying, "God, conform me now. Do whatever You need to do this morning, this day, throughout this week to remove whatever needs to be gone in my life, anything in my life that would hinder me from becoming what You want me to be."

God can use anything. Can He use cancer in your life to chip it away? Yes. Can He use the loss of a job? Yes. He also can use good things that come into our lives, but I think the trials have more of an effect on the finished product. God is more concerned about what He's doing *in* you than around you and through you—because it's not about you. The more people see you, the less they see Christ. If there is no change in you, there's no Jesus in you. As you allow Christ to change you, His image is going to start being reflected in the way you live, work, or play.

When you look in the mirror, do you see more of Christ than you saw a year ago, two years ago, ten years ago? God is chipping away what doesn't belong there and transforming you into the image of Christ. As I get older and as I become more like God, more of the appetites, the glory, the thinking, and the abnormalities of the world go away.

How Are We Transformed?

Through an intimate relationship with Christ (Ph 3:7–10). The more we grow in an intimate relationship with Christ, the more we will take on His character and become like Him. The more we get to know Him, the more we love Him and become like Him.

By hiding His Word in our hearts (Ps 119:11). Hebrews 4:12 calls the Bible a "double-edged sword." As God chips away at us, it may hurt sometimes, but it is vital that we allow God's word to dwell in our hearts and begin to get rid of what doesn't belong.

Through prayer (Ma 6:1–13). As we confess our sins to God and interact with Him through prayer, He brings things to our minds and hearts that gently transform us by His cleansing power.

Through the renewing of our mind, heart, soul, and strength (Ro 12:2). Stinking thinking leads to lousy living. God wants to give us the mind of Christ. When our innermost thoughts dwell on things that are true, noble, right, and pure (Ph 4:8), our actions spring out of those thoughts. The more our minds are conformed to Christ's, the more our actions will be also.

By denying ourselves (Ph 3:10). This goes against every instinct— we don't like to deny ourselves. If I want a piece of pie, I go get it. If I see an advertisement for a new tool, I can run right down to the store and buy it. The world has made it easy to indulge ourselves, but being conformed to the image of Christ requires that we deny ourselves the things that don't benefit us eternally. When we say no to ourselves, God can use that to chip away at us.

Through our personal trials and testing (Ga 2:20). Trials are a major influence in the transformation process. Even things that seem negative—the loss of a job, a sudden illness, a personal disaster—can be good if they are used to chisel away the attitudes and actions that do not reflect Christ. God will turn the trials around and make them into something good because He is more concerned about what He is doing in you than with you and through you.

By continually yielding to the leading of the Holy Spirit (2 Co 3:18). Paul wrote very clearly, *"Do not grieve the Holy Spirit"* (Ep 4:30). The Holy Spirit is not a loud yell. He is a still, small voice that we must listen for carefully. Our job is to yield to the Spirit and allow Him to chisel off parts of our lives that don't belong. Every day there are areas in my life where I still have to yield. Even as our world is yelling at us to conform, we have to say "no" and turn to the Word and prayer, allowing the Holy Spirit to work in us.

By humbling ourselves (Ph 2:1–11). Paul said, *"Whatever was to my profit I now consider loss for the sake of Christ"* (Ph 3:7). Just as Jesus humbled himself by becoming a human in His own creation, we must humble ourselves if we are going to become like Him. This is the exact opposite of what the world tells us to do, but it is necessary if we want to be conformed to Christ's image.

Through divine encounters (Jo 4). When you get in a car accident or something breaks down around the house, do you see God in the situation? When you've had the worst possible day, do you ask yourself how God might be trying to speak to you? Divine encounters can be disguised as the most everyday occurrences. The difference is that we are open to God's chisel working in our lives.

By becoming a bondservant (Jo 13). Remember, a bondservant serves not under compulsion, but out of love. It's not about us, our pride, or what we want. It's about what Christ wants. Just as Jesus came to do the will of the Father, the more we submit to God's will, the more He is able to chip away. I want Him to be able to mold me into Christ's image as I submit to God, and I say, "God, I'm your servant. Do whatever You will. Do whatever You need to do, because I want it to be about You."

When your life is characterized by the transforming work of God, you will be able to say to others, as Paul said, "Follow me as I follow Christ." That's what my dad showed me. He never had much in resources, but he showed me the way to the cross, and it was at the cross that I found the changed life.

When I was youngster, I saw a cocoon (chrysalis) on a log. One half of the wings were showing. It was beautiful. I thought it would be good if I could help that butterfly come out. So I took my pocket knife and gradually opened up the cocoon, expecting to find another beautiful wing—only to discover a "gooey mess."

I learned a lesson from that now-expired butterfly. The only way God can change us is from the inside out. He will use people, circumstances, and things from the outside to conform us to His will and purpose, but real transformation takes place in our hearts, souls, and minds. Don't try to fix people. Let the Holy Spirit do that. Our responsibility is to refuse to conform to this world. Allow the Holy Spirit to transform you into the image of Jesus Christ, and a year from now you are going to look more like Christ. Then you can be "like God in the flesh."

Imagine the possibilities!

MOVING TOWARD MY "GREATER YES!"

1. What does God need to chisel away in my life?

2. What is God using to chisel it away?

3. What am I doing to resist God's work in my life?

4. What am I doing to submit to God's work in my life?

5. What have I learned that will help me move toward my "Greater Yes!"?

MY PRAYER OF COMMITMENT

Gracious Father, thank You for sending Your Son to die for me. I recognize that the world is trying to conform me to its principles, and I want instead to be transformed by You into the image of Your Son. I want to live my new life by new principles. Help me get into the process of the potential You promised. Amen.

⁓ CHAPTER 17 ⁓

Requires a Greater Dependency

God wants to create in you a higher level of dependency.

For eleven years, I studied diligently to earn a little piece of paper called a Doctorate of Ministry (D.Min.). After I received it, my nine-year-old son summed it up well as he ran around the church telling everyone, "My dad has a de-mon!"

I worked eleven years to get that "demon," and in the end I was the same person that I was before. The reason was that I found confidence in having that degree rather than having complete confidence in my relationship with God.

The Word of God never speaks of self-confidence or self-esteem. Those are terms given to us by the world. However, the Bible does talk about godly confidence. You can have godly confidence without being self-confident.

When a child grows up knowing that his father wants nothing to do with him, he could easily grow up with a lack of self-confidence and feel devalued. When I have the opportunity to work with single mothers, I tell their kids what I tell my grandkids, "You are the best, because God says you're the best." I don't want them to become egotistical and overly self-confident, but I do want them to develop a godly confidence from knowing their worth as God's children, no matter what they're going through.

What things do you put your confidence in? Proverbs 3 5–6 says, *Trust in the LORD with all your heart and lean not on your own understanding; in all your ways acknowledge him, and he will make your paths straight.*

Everything I learned during my studies in college and seminary has been extremely valuable to me personally, and I'm glad I have my doctorate. But in comparison to knowing Jesus Christ, it's all worthless (Ph 3).

What are some of the things in our society that bring confidence? Money, position, titles, abilities and strengths, good looks, being married, family background—all these things give us self-confidence. Some of us also find confidence in the government, our economy, the church, and other people.

Here is a fill-in-the-blank test: If ___(Example: My Money)___ were gone, how much confidence would I have? Fill in the blank with the thing that brings you the most confidence in this world. If your money were gone, how much confidence would you have? If your business were gone, how much confidence would you have? If your health were gone, how much confidence would you have? If your position were gone, how much confidence would you have?

One time I stayed up all night praying. Actually, my wife calls it worry-prayer. I pray, then I worry, then I pray, then I worry some more, because I get fearful. Sometimes in the midst of a trial, I find myself filled with fear because my confidence is misplaced. I have to stop and ask myself, "What am I putting my confidence in? Is it my position? Is it in my ministry? Is it what people say about me?"

For most of my early life, people didn't say a lot of good things about me because I could barely hear and I couldn't speak at all. Even after my hearing was fixed, I still heard their negative comments. I determined to build up my self-confidence so I wouldn't believe what they said. But I was listening to the wrong god. Finally somebody told me, "You need to go to God's Word and hear what God says about you. God says you're the best. You're made in His image. Nobody can take that away from you."

Your Godly Confidence + Your Faith = Greater Dependency

Godly Confidence vs. Self-Confidence

You don't need self-confidence to have confidence in the Lord, because it's not about you. There are some significant differences between godly confidence and self-confidence.

It's a matter of provision. Who or what are you depending on to meet your needs? Your paycheck? The security of money in the bank? Godly confidence means relying on the Lord not only for our spiritual needs, but for our physical ones as well.

It's a matter of trust. When you're in trouble, to whom do you look for deliverance? Do you trust yourself to take hold of the situation and get back on your feet again? Or do you immediately run to God and put your cares at his feet? Self-confidence says, "I can do it"; godly confidence says, "God can do it."

It's a matter of dependency. Who or what do you depend on to get through life? I've known believers who got through their week by clinging to a can of beer—the buzz it gives them helps keep them moving. Were they still Christians? Yes, but they didn't have a godly confidence.

It's a matter of relationship. What or who makes you happy? Happiness is often based on happenings—as long as the happenings are great, then we're happy. Can we have joy when we're not happy? Yes, if our joy is found in the Lord.

It's a matter of security. Where does your family find security? Right now, if you have kids, they probably find security in you, knowing you provide and care for them. But where is your security? Most people, if they would really admit it, would probably say, "In the bank," or "My nice house and things." The problem is that all those things can fail us. Godly confidence means trust in the security of a relationship with the one who never fails us.

It's a matter of significance. In what are you seeking meaning and purpose? Most people find significance in what they have accomplished or what other people say about them. If they hear constant criticism and negativity, they think that is what they are. The wonderful thing about having godly confidence is that God always has good things to say about you—He loves you and is pleased with you because you are His!

It's a matter of perspective. Where is your focus? As long as Peter had his eyes on the Lord, he didn't sink. But when he looked at the circumstances and the storm around him, be began to falter. What you see determines what you feel, which determines what you do. If you have confidence in God, you will see His hand working, and you will trust Him for the results.

It's a matter of passion. Where do you spend your time, your talent, and your treasure? Where your heart is, that's where your confidence will be. You can say you are confident in the Lord, but do you show it by the way you invest your time, talent, and treasure—the things that are most valuable to you? That is what really determines where your passion is.

God's Power + Godly Confidence = "Your 'Greater Yes!"

Exchanging Self-Confidence for Godly Confidence

One of the great biblical examples of a man who possessed godly confidence is King David. The story of David and Goliath beautifully illustrates godly confidence.

In 1 Samuel 17:26, David is speaking to the Israelite army. He says: *"Who is this uncircumcised Philistine that he should defy the armies of the living God?"* Good question.

David's words were reported to King Saul, who immediately sent for him. Saul said to David, *You are not able to go out against this Philistine and fight him; you are only a boy, and he has been a fighting man from his youth* (v. 33).

Here's what David's godly confidence enabled him to say:

> *"Your servant has killed both the lion and the bear; this uncircumcised Philistine will be like one of them, because he has defied the armies of the living God. The Lord who delivered me from the paw of the lion and the paw of the bear will deliver me from the hand of this Philistine."*
>
> 1 Samuel 17:36–37

So Saul pulled out his own armor and began to put it on David. Since Saul had confidence in his armor, he wanted to give it to David. However, besides the fact that David could barely walk with all that heavy armor on him, he didn't find his confidence in it. Instead, he went and found five smooth stones and took out his slingshot.

David approached Goliath and said: *"You come against me with sword and spear and javelin, but I come against you in the name of the Lord Almighty, the God of the armies of Israel, whom you have defied"* (v. 45). He understood that the enemy was coming at them with self-confidence because of their wealth, power, and strength. Unfortunately for them, David had confidence in God's ability to deliver Israel.

When I lived among the Native Americans, I often watched them make and use slings. They would cut a piece of leather and attach two strings on each end, and they could do everything with it from knocking a bird out of the air to killing a jackrabbit. So I know slings really work. David took one of his stones and slung it at Goliath. If I were facing a giant with only a sling and a stone, I would be standing there trembling. But David took his godly confidence and put it into action. He dropped Goliath to the ground, and then beheaded the giant with his own sword.

Wouldn't you love to have the confidence David had? It is possible when we exchange our self-confidence for godly confidence. Here's how:

It starts with an intimate relationship. You cannot develop confidence in someone you do not know. Even a brief read through the Psalms will show you David knew God intimately. He relied on God for the present and trusted Him for the future because he had witnessed His faithfulness in the past. There is no way David could have known God would fight the battle for him if he had not spent time with his Father. In Psalm 42:1, David prayed: *As the deer pants for streams of water, so my soul pants for you, O God.* If you want godly confidence, start your day by thirsting after a relationship with God.

It involves personal experience. David didn't jump right into fighting giants. First he learned to keep the foxes away from the sheep, and then he killed a lion and a bear. As he experienced God's power in the small things, he gradually trusted Him for more and more. You cannot develop godly confidence without personal experience.

It develops through testing. You cannot battle with weapons you've never tested. David wasn't familiar with Saul's armor. The world will hand you a whole array of armor and say, "Do battle with this armor," but it won't work for spiritual battles. God's Word tells us what we need: the helmet of salvation, the breastplate of righteousness, the shield of faith, the sword of the Spirit (the Bible), and the belt of truth (Ep 6:10–17).

It demands courage. No one said it would be easy, but God will use what He has given you. Whether it's your lunch, as with the boy with the five loaves and two fish, or your slingshot, as with David, God will take what you have and use it. Have courage in your godly confidence.

It requires clear focus. Don't let the enemy intimidate you and bring fear. He will whisper lies: "You're too young," "You're too old," "You're worthless," "You're not good enough." Don't listen! Godly confidence requires that we focus on the truths of the Lord. He's our provider, our strong tower, our shield and our strength, our fortress and deliverer—it is Him we trust! Keep your focus on God's word and what it says about you and about the One in whom you have confidence.

It requires that you let go. God will not take you somewhere if He has not already gone before you. You just have to let go of the security of what you're holding onto and put your confidence in His abilities, not your own. We have to let go of our self-confidence to find godly confidence. David had to let go of the sling to kill Goliath.

It results in personal victory. The battle is the Lord's, and He will give it into our hands. I don't know what your battle is, but I do know the victory lies in Him. When we have godly confidence, we will always come out winners in the end.

Cathy and I have learned if we are going to do great things for God, fulfill our "Greater Yes!", we have to have a greater dependency upon God. We know there are giants ahead of us, and we cannot face them on our own. In fact, we love to go out to dinner and celebrate what God is going to do.

I am reminded again of a time on the reservation when we had completely run out of food. My mom gathered all us kids in the kitchen and as we ate our last bowls of rice, we prayed together and thanked God for what He was going to do. Believing God would answer our prayer, the next day we all got up expecting to find bags of groceries on our doorstep, and we did. It is too bad I grew up. I am glad I am thinking and trusting like a kid again.

In order to develop your "Greater Yes!", you need to depend more on God and less on yourself. I do not fear failure; I fear succeeding at something that does not matter. Where are we putting our confidence? If it is in ourselves, it will bring no eternal value. Eternity is a long time. If the thing you put your confidence in were gone, what would sustain you and your family? That's the very thing you've got to let go of. This lifetime is nothing compared to eternity, and only godly confidence will help us win the battles that will impact our eternal destiny.

Imagine the possibilities!

MOVING TOWARD MY "GREATER YES!"

1. What would I do for God if I had all the resources I needed?

2. What is God creating in me that can only be provided by Him?

3. What am I depending on or looking to, to meet my daily needs?

4. What would it take for me to trust God for my "Greater Yes!"?

5. What have I learned that will help me move toward my "Greater Yes!"?

MY PRAYER OF COMMITMENT

Heavenly Father, thank You for the example in David's life of godly confidence. Help me let go of the things I put confidence in here on earth and begin to develop confidence in You alone. Help me to know that the battle is Yours and to look to You for my confidence. My confidence is in You alone. Amen.

⸙ CHAPTER 18 ⸙

Raising Your Level of Expectancy

God will always exceed your level of expectancy.

If you suddenly got that new job you've been wanting for years, how would it change your life? If you received a million dollars tomorrow, how would it change your potential? If you found your "Greater Yes!" today, how would that change your expectations of God?

Your "Greater Yes!" + Your Faith = Greater Expectancy

We like to dream about great things happening to us, even when it seems improbable. But did you know God can change your life in the midst of where you're at right now? We're always looking for change to come, when all along God is waiting, ready to work in our lives.

If you expect defeat, failure, or mediocrity, your mind, soul, heart, and spirit will make sure you sabotage every attempt to achieve your "Greater Yes!" However, if you are committed with your mind, soul, heart, and spirit to succeed at what really matters, you can achieve your "Greater Yes!"

A couple of years ago when I was lying in that hospital bed, God began to teach me that I needed to rise to a whole new level of expectancy. I was limiting what God wanted to do in and through my life. I knew his will was that I focus on the development of People Matter Ministries. But instead of looking to Him to be the supernatural source and resource for the fulfillment of His will, I tried to make His will happen within my abilities, my income, and my circumstances. Trying to fulfill a divine call with only human effort landed me in the hospital.

Before the prophet Elijah was taken up to heaven, he asked his protégé Elisha, "What can I do for you before I am taken from you?" Elisha replied, "Let me inherit a double portion of your spirit" (2 Ki 2:9). Oh, if I had only prayed likewise.

I believe God is asking us the same question. Do you think God doesn't want to give us a double portion of His blessing? Why do we settle for less? In Luke 11:9, Jesus Christ promised us, *"Ask and it will be given to you; seek and you will find; knock and the door will be opened to you."*

The assumption is that we are asking according to God's will, not ours. This verse doesn't promise that if we ask for material stuff he will always give it to us Jesus continued,

> *Which of you fathers, if your son asks for a fish, will give him a snake instead? Or if he asks for an egg, will give him a scorpion? If you then, though you are evil, know how to give good gifts to your children, how much more will your Father in heaven give the Holy Spirit to those who ask him!*
>
> Luke 11:11-13

God wants us to bring our needs to Him. But we need to remember that, unlike us, God sees the whole picture. So often when we say, "God, give me your blessing," we're thinking of a nice house and a new car in the garage. We're thinking of now, not eternity. But God knows what we need, and He can see how giving us what we ask for will affect the rest of our lives.

A man may plead for a mate, get married, then discover she is not exactly whom he thought he married, and conclude he married a snake. But God knows that leaning on him and persevering through marital woes will yield more Christ-like character, and *that's* the big fish. God is handing us a fish, but it may look like a snake. Sometimes God will allow us to go through some difficult things in order to strengthen our dependency on Him and raise our level of expectancy of Him.

I don't want to live a life that just fits in—a life that neatly mirrors society's shallow values. I want to live a life that echoes in eternity! If God is willing to give me a double portion of His Spirit, I'm going to ask for it.

Why Should God Give Us the Best?

I believe God can give us the best because He believes the best in us. In order to gain a higher level of expectancy, we need to gain a deeper understanding of our own worth. You have great worth to God. That's why He sent His Son to die for you. Understanding our worth to God leads us to a deeper level of intimacy with Him. When we understand our worth, it drives us to want to be with God. I like hanging out with someone who likes me. God likes you and me!

A deeper understanding of our intimacy leads us to a deeper level of dependency on God. This is about me—I cannot do it alone. Then, a deeper understanding of our dependency leads to a deeper level of inadequacy. As much as we wish we could run our own lives, we have to realize we are completely in need of God.

Next, a deeper understanding of our inadequacy leads to a deeper level of humility. When we get driven down, we get raised up by God, and a deeper understanding of our humility leads to a higher level of greatness. So, we actually descend according to the world's view. But, in fact, by letting go of all the dead weight of caring for material success and social climbing, like a spiritual helium balloon powered by the unseen, we rise to greatness. It's when you go low that you become great. Christ said, *"The greatest among you should be like the youngest, and the one who rules like the one who serves"* (Lk 22:26).

A deeper understanding of true greatness leads to a higher level of possibilities. Once we resign from the rat race, God can begin to show us unlimited possibilities. Finally, a deeper understanding of our possibilities leads us to a higher level of expectancy. Now I am prepared to receive from God more than I could ever ask.

Great Expectations Bear Great Fruit

As our expectations of God increase, we will grow in other areas of our lives.

Greater hope. What do you put your hope in? Is it your job, your health, your money? I love the old hymn that says, "My hope is built on nothing less than Jesus' blood and righteousness." When you begin to rise to a higher level of expectancy, your hope is no longer in all that other stuff; your hope is in God.

Greater dependency. Expectancy will require that we let go and depend on God for everything. Our level of expectancy is in direct proportion to our level of trust.

Greater faith. Faith is the *evidence of things not seen* (He 11:1 NKJV). What are you asking God for that you can't see? Can you imagine great things for your future? Don't limit your expectations by your own personal capacity or resources. (This is the voice of experience speaking!)

Greater obedience. Obedience is faith in action. When I lay in the hospital, God was saying to me, "Dan, quit being disobedient. I told you to do something and you're not doing it because you lack faith. You won't obey me; you won't trust me." I have been learning that being obedient allows me to expect even greater things from God.

Greater confidence. Why did David pick up five stones when he went to face Goliath? Do you think he was afraid he would miss? That's what the average person would say, because we like to have a backup plan just in case God doesn't come through. I believe David had more faith than that—perhaps he took four other stones because the giant had four brothers and he was going to nail them, too. Of course, he never had to since they all fled after the first one went down. We don't need a backup plan when we have a greater expectancy.

Greater peace. God gives us a peace that surpasses all comprehension. People will say, "I can't believe you can be so calm in the middle of what you're going through! How could you be at peace amid such turmoil?" It's because you have a higher level of expectancy. You know God is going to come through for you.

Greater love. The Bible says that perfect love casts out fear. My little grandson fell the other day coming out of a restaurant, and he began to cry, so I went over and picked him up and hugged him. It wasn't long before he stopped. I think God wants us to go to Him occasionally and just cry if we need to. He wants to put His arm around us and comfort us. He wants us to fall in love with him, because that's part of expecting amazing things from Him.

What to Expect?

When you have a higher level of expectancy, expect miracles! God is just waiting for you to ask.

Expect things to change in your favor. Expect to have the power to survive life's challenges. Look forward to them with expectancy. Get up in the morning and say, "Bring it on. Come my way if you dare." Don't say it with cockiness, but say it with godly confidence, knowing the power is not you, but is within you because of what Christ has done. When Satan attacks, ignore his lies. Listen for God's still, small voice.

Expect God to meet you at your level of expectancy. If you'll start expecting more of God, God will meet you there. He's ready and waiting. As you study His Word, you'll begin to understand what God is saying, and it will cause you to raise your level of faith and expectancy. If you do not expect things to get better, they probably won't. God is not the problem; our doubt is the only thing holding us back. Belief and release is not based on the amount of my faith but the focus on my faith. It is in God.

Expect that good things are coming your way. This is not just positive thinking, this is proper thinking. By good things, I mean things that conform you to the image of Jesus. Expect God's goodness to come your way. We tie God's hands because of our own unbelief, not realizing that what we receive is directly connected to what we believe God will bring in and through us.

Expect to see your potential through the eyes of faith. Ask God to help you begin to understand His will for you. We need to get out of the cocoon Satan has deceived us into. God has decreed an incredible potential, dream, and purpose for each of us, but He requires that we can look through eyes of faith. We will move toward what we see and believe in our minds and hearts.

Expect the favor and blessing of God. I expect God to bless me. In fact, I get up in the morning and say, "God bless me this day, and even more importantly, make me a blessing." We must believe God loves and is pleased with us and wants to bless us. What you can believe and expect of God according to His will, will be blessed.

Expect to become a dream giver. I highly recommend the book by Bruce Wilkinson entitled *The Dream Giver*. It has helped thousands of people understand the path to their dreams. It has helped me immensely. My calling is to help men and women find their "Greater Yes!" and give them a dream. That greater dependency has given me a greater expectancy for what God can and will do through me in the lives of those I minister to.

When Cathy and I started People Matter Ministries in January 2005, we had little clue what we were doing or where God was taking us. God clearly called us off our map and onto His compass. A map gives you clear direction with details. I am all male, but I like asking directions. When God told us to go north to start PMM, I wanted all the details. I wanted to know how we were going to manage it, staff it, and pay for it.

The problem with preaching is that we are tested by our own words. I have asked hundreds of people, "If you had unlimited re-

sources and complete freedom to fail, what would you do for God?"
Then God turned my words around and asked me, "Since I have given
you unlimited resources and complete freedom to fail, what would
you expect of God? Please don't limit your God by expecting too little. Don't limit your expectations of your God by your own limited capacity and resources. This is not about you, but about God. Remember I am God and you are not."

So Cathy and I decided to go for it. With the help of our closest
friends, we have discovered a master plan designed by God, and it will
require that He show up or it will be impossible to do. I love being
where we are. I know God will meet us at our level of expectancy.

Expectancy is simply anticipating from God more than you can
ever think or imagine. What do you have to lose?

Imagine the possibilities!

MOVING TOWARD MY "GREATER YES!"

1. What has been my typical level of expectancy toward God?
   Why?

2. If I knew I had unlimited resources and complete freedom to
   fail, what would I expect from God?

3. What am I allowing in my life that is limiting what God wants
   to do in, with, and through me?

4. What am I doing currently that is being blessed by God?

5. What have I learned that will help me move toward my
   "Greater Yes!"?

MY PRAYER OF COMMITMENT

Father, thank You that You want to take me places that I have never dreamed of. And You want to use me in greater ways than I could ever imagine. Thank You that what You have in store for me goes beyond my own capacity and ability. I will not allow worry, fret, my job, my health, anything in my life to rob me of my God-given potential. Amen.

CHAPTER 19

Receive Power Through Your Thoughts and Words

*God wants to turn your thoughts and words into power
for your potential.*

Someone once told me, "People will not necessarily remember what you do or say, but they will always remember how you made them feel."

One of the questions I have wrestled with is: Do thoughts and words really hurt? You've heard the saying, "Sticks and stones may break my bones, but words will never hurt me." Well, that's a lie. Our words can make others feel a hurt they will never forget.

One day when my daughter was in middle school she brought home a paper with a zero on it. She had misunderstood the assignment and for her efforts was given a zero. She said to me, "Why did I even try?" It made her feel like zero. Thoughts and words have the power to either immobilize or propel us to our potential. The teacher missed an incredible opportunity to teach grace and mercy by allowing her a "do-over." Praise God, He does allow do-overs!

There is a battle between the spirit of life and the spirit of death inside each of us (Ep 2:1–7). We have the power to express life or death through our thoughts and words. God wants to give us the mind of Christ because He knows that if He can change our thinking, it will change our feelings and, consequently, our actions. Jesus Christ said,

It is not what enters into the mouth that defiles the man but what proceeds out of the mouth, this defiles the man...But the things that proceed out of the mouth come from the heart, and those defile the man. For out of the heart come evil thoughts, murders, adulteries, fornications, thefts, false witness, slanders. These are the things which defile the man; but to eat with unwashed hands does not defile the man.

(Ma 15:11, 18–20 NASB)

What we put into our minds will go into our hearts and then come out of our mouths. That's why we have to be so careful. David prayed in Psalm 19:14: *May the words of my mouth and the meditation of my heart be pleasing in your sight, O LORD.* Our thoughts and words together equal our potential. Thoughts are the *essence* of our heart, soul, mind, and strength; they are what God uses to change us from within. Our words, then, are the *expression* of our heart, soul, mind, and strength, and our actions are the *results* of what is expressed by the essence of our heart, soul, mind, and strength.

Because we were made in the image of God, we were born to create. Thoughts and words have the power to create. We can create vision, anticipation, and hope with our words; we can help bring the best out of people through our words. We can build up or tear down.

I had a friend who introduced one of his children as his "prodigal son." I asked him later, "Why do you introduce him that way? You are speaking destiny into his heart." Our words can speak potential and destiny in the hearts of people. Your words should express your expectations for others. That is why I tell my grandkids they are the best. I remind them that since they are the best, they need to live out who they are.

When you or your boss walks into the room, how do people feel? Do they say, "That guy really energizes me," or do they say, "I always feel depressed after he says something." It reminds me of Pigpen in the comic strip Peanuts; wherever he goes a cloud of dust surrounds him. What surrounds you? Does your presence encourage others to contribute?

Your Thoughts + Your Words = Unleashes God's Power

The Power of Our Thoughts

Hear what Paul wrote in Philippians 4:8: *Finally, brothers, whatever is true, whatever is noble, whatever is right, whatever is pure, whatever is lovely, whatever is admirable—if anything is excellent or praiseworthy— think about such things.*

The Greek word that we translate "meditate" actually means "to chew on"—the way a cow chews her cud. She slowly and deliberately chews the food over and over again. These are some of the things God wants us to "chew on":

Whatever is true. What is true about you? What is truthful in your character? I don't enjoy being told I'm wrong, but if that is true, sooner or later I need to hear it. Sometimes the truth hurts. If we put aside ego and our good opinion of ourselves, we also find truth about ourselves in the Word of God.

Whatever is noble. Nobility implies integrity in all you do. When we honor God with our thinking, we push out that which is not noble. While Satan wants to give us a divided mind, integrity is noble, and means being whole and complete.

Whatever is right. We need to dwell on things that are righteous and holy. Will evil thoughts still come? Of course, but we need to take those captive. (2 Co 10:5) How? Refuse to mediate on those things that are not profitable or beneficial to your family, marriage, or your walk with God.

Whatever is pure. I tell men who have a problem with pornography, "Fall in love so much with God that you won't want things that separate you from Him." God knows the inner pain you try to mask with perverse excitement; He will fill your emptiness with His Spirit. Then, the light of God's loving forgiveness and acceptance will heal the hurt and self-loathing that formerly swirled in dark recesses of your being. God will give you confidence, in Christ, so that you may say: *I will not set before my eyes anything that is base. I hate the work of those who fall away; it shall not cleave to me. Perverseness of heart shall be far from me; I will know nothing of evil* (Ps 101:3-4, RSV).

Whatever is lovely. When you look at people, do you seek the best in them? Can you see the best in yourself? The other day a guy gave me a whole list of things wrong with his wife. I told him that was the wrong approach! We need to look at God's Word and see what it says about us. Instead of fixating on the bad qualities, let's choose to look for what is lovely and thank God for it.

Whatever is admirable. The NASB renders Philippians 4:8, as "Whatever is of good repute." What is fit for God to hear? If you wouldn't want to start up a conversation with God about it, don't let it in your head!

Whatever is excellent or praiseworthy. What would God call "excellent"? What things are fit to be praised? There are so many wonderful things about God that by the time we're done listing them, there won't be any time left to think of the things that don't deserve praise.

As we begin to put the right stuff in our heads, we also need to *take captive every thought to make it obedient to Christ* (2 Co 10:5). What do we put in our minds on a daily basis? What are you listening to on the radio on the way to work? What are you watching on TV? What are you reading? What are you meditating upon? Our thoughts determine our words and actions.

The Power of Our Words

Ephesians 4:29, 31 says: *Do not let any unwholesome talk come out of your mouths, but only what is helpful for building others up according to their needs, that it may benefit those who listen. Get rid of all bitterness, rage and anger, brawling and slander, along with every form of malice.* There's a cause and effect in these verses—if our words come out and they're not godly and edifying, then they come from the seeds of bitterness, anger, and slander.

Do people see God because they hear our words? Do they feel God because we're in their presence? The following are some of the words we need to speak:

Wholesome words. Unwholesome words are rotten fruit. I went to buy some oranges the other day, and I noticed one rotten orange at the bottom of the pile that was rotting all the others around it. I threw that rotten, corrupting orange out. I could tell you every day for twenty years that you are God's best. Then one day I could say something rotten to you that would spoil out those twenty years in an instant. That's why we have to be so careful with our words.

Appropriate words. Appropriate words speak to the needs of the moment. We can say words that are right but inappropriate.

Encouraging words. These bespeak the best of others and build them up.

Truthful words. Basically, don't lie. Even when they are difficult, you can find truthful words to show someone that which needs to be seen, without crushing their spirit in the process.

Transforming words. Our words should edify others and transform their environments.

Forgiving words. Because God has forgiven us, we need to forgive others. After teaching the disciples the Lord's Prayer, Jesus told them this: "For if you forgive men when they sin against you, your heavenly

Father will also forgive you. But if you do not forgive men their sins, your Father will not forgive your sins" *(Ma 6:14-15)*. How do you treat those who have offended you? Are you satisfied if God treats you the same way?

Thankful words. Do you thank your spouse for the little things he or she does? Do you thank your friends for caring about you? Every one needs to hear thankful words, including God.

_____ **words.** What are the words that you need to speak? Joyful words? Exciting words? Challenging words? You fill in the blank. As you think about your home, work, and church, what kind of words do you need to be speaking?

Our words reveal the essence of our heart, soul, mind, and strength. Galatians 5:22–23 lists the *fruit of the Spirit* that should characterize our actions: love, joy, peace, patience, kindness, goodness, faithfulness, gentleness, and self-control. Do your words reflect these?

It is by the fruit of our thoughts, words, and behavior that we are known. Together, the fruit of your thinking and actions propel you to your potential.

The Power of Our Potential

> *Garbage In—Garbage Out*
> *Truth In—Truth Out*

Your potential is conditional to what you allow your mind to dwell on, because that affects your actions.

If you will control your thoughts and your words, you can change your world. One day I was going through the drive-thru at the coffee shop while talking on my cell phone. The young man was trying to take my order while I was tossing money at him and trying to continue my phone conversation. Later, as I drove away with my latte, God said to me, "You were rude. That is one of my creations, and you were rude to him."

So I drove back to the shop and went in and asked for the young man at the window and apologized. I knew I could have put my phone conversation on hold or waited until I was finished to go through and get my coffee, but I was only thinking of myself. The next time I went there, I made sure I wasn't on the phone.

My actions were the result of my thoughts. I was busy doing my own thing—so busy that I ignored the feelings of a young man. Your potential is conditional to what you allow to come into your mind, and how you express it through your words and your behavior. I wonder how much potential I have lost because of my words and my thoughts. But I'm not dead yet—I can change. I want to learn to control my thoughts and words so I can change my world.

Don't allow bitterness, anger, worry, or busyness to rob you of your God-given potential. Our thoughts, words, and actions are powerful forces that can change our world if we use them for the edification of others. Proper thinking leads to proper speaking which leads to powerful potential. God wants to change your words and your thoughts because he wants you to reach your "Greater Yes!"

Imagine the possibilities!

MOVING TOWARD MY "GREATER YES!"

1. What am I allowing to come into my mind?

2. What is the focus of my thoughts?

3. How would I classify my words? Do they edify or defile?

4. What am I thinking and speaking about myself? Others?

5. What have I learned that will help me move toward my "Greater Yes!"?

MY PRAYER OF COMMITMENT

Father, thank You for the ability to think and speak. Let the mediations of my heart be pleasing in Your sight. I will not allow   (Example: Doubt)   to be planted in my thoughts to rob me of my God-given potential. I will not allow my speech to rob others of their God-given potential. I will seek to match my behavior with what I believe in my heart, think in my mind, and say with my words, by Your power within me. Amen.

CHAPTER 20

Find Strength from Adversities and Difficulties

God allows adversities and difficulties in your life according to your need.

My coach used to tell me, "If you run another lap, it will hurt so good." At the time I thought he was nuts—how can something "hurt good?" But in many ways it's true.

Most of us would not wish for adversities and difficulties. On the contrary, we ask questions like, "Why me, Lord?" What we don't realize is that sometimes our trials can "hurt so good" if we accept them and look for what God is doing with us through them.

The key thing I've learned about difficulties and trials is that God is more concerned about how he's changing us than how he's changing our circumstances. It is more about the journey than the destination. If I'm saying, "God, do whatever You need to do to conform Your image in me," then I can't start whining when difficulties come into my life. God is simply answering my prayer.

So why does God allow adversities and difficulties? Romans 8:28 says: *In all things God works for the good of those who love him, who have been called according to his purpose.* Are there any exceptions? No. *All things* means: our job situations, our marriages, our finances, even our physical ailments and our addictions. Even my own sin, my own mistakes, God can use for my good because He can work through those things to conform me into the very image of His Son.

God allows difficulties and trials according to our need. Behind every trial, every difficulty, every problem, every obstacle I face, there is an unmet need that God is trying to reveal to me. I say, "God, show me what You need to do in my life. Do whatever You need to do," and then He begins to expose my need and my weakness.

God tests us because he already knows what He's going to do. He tests our faith, our character, our endurance—and He shows us what we are really made of. When He squeezes, He brings out that person that He wants us to become. It shows you where your weaknesses are, where you need more of His power, and where His Spirit needs more of you.

God reveals what or whom we're depending on. What are you looking to that you believe will deliver you from your difficulties and your adversities? If you're not running straight to God, He will have to squeeze harder until you realize that you need Him alone.

God desires that you have His best of your life now. Sometimes God hands me a bowl of peas. I hate peas. My mother used to tell me that they're "God's candy," and I still hated them. But they are good for me, and God knows I need what is good for me more than I need what I like.

Your Adversities + Your Difficulties + Vision = Your Potential

A Proper View of Adversity

Let's look again at that important passage from Jesus:

> *"Which of you fathers, if your son asks for a fish, will give him a snake instead? Or if he asks for an egg, will give him a scorpion? If you then, though you are evil, know how to give good gifts to your children, how much more will your Father in heaven give the Holy Sprit to those who ask him!"*
>
> Luke 11:11–13

Cathy has a friend whose ex-husband keeps dragging her into court. He does not keep his word, aggravates their children, and is a thorn in her flesh. The biggest problem is how she views the man. She sees her ex-husband as a snake instead of fish, a scorpion instead of an egg. She cannot see that her ex could be the provision the Heavenly Father is using to make her the person He wants her to be. How do you view adversities and difficulties? Do you see them through the eyes of your heart or the eyes of your head? In order for the Holy Spirit to get involved, you have to see adversity through the eyes of your heart. When God allows a trial in your life, He does it because He loves you and He knows that learning to lay your burdens down at God's feet will help make you into the image of Jesus, who trusted God even when God made Him understand that doing so would cost His very life. Difficulties given over in prayer to God in trusting faith create in the believer a higher level of dependency, which moves us to a higher level of expectancy.

What do you see when your boss is coming toward you? What do you see when that trial appears? What do you see when you go home to a wife who has three kids crawling all over her and is ready to fall apart? What you see really determines what you feel, which determines what you do.

A great stack of lumber sits on a leveled lot. Mindful of material values, one man sees it and thinks of the staggering cost of the boards, losing value as it sits exposed to the elements in a muddy field. Another man, perceiving through his own base personal interests, sees only a great number of splinters he will get if he has to handle it. Neither man can see beyond the fact of a pile of boards; nor have they interpreted that fact in a way that brings glory to God. We must see through the eyes of faith, because we make decisions based on what we see. Accepting that some boards may warp before they can be used and workmen may get splinters, we must see beyond the petty annoyances of the here and now. Viewing that same lumber through the eyes of faith, we can know that with God's help a house can be built that will stand handsome and sturdy for years to come.

Although we can and should continue to ask God for deliverance, we also need to trust His timing. Our instinct would be to say, "God, deliver me, and do it now." God replies, "No, you need to be chiseled out a little while." He uses difficulties and adversity to chisel away what does not belong in our lives. "You need to be squeezed a little bit." When you are squeezed, what comes out—the flesh or the spirit? God squeezes us according to our need.

God is concerned about the process of transforming us into the image of His Son. As He does that, we should look for His provision through our adversity and difficulty.

How are you facing your adversities and difficulties? Most Christians run from them. However, God is telling us those three words no athlete wants to hear: "Take another lap," because He knows it will hurt so good.

You can run from your adversity, you can run from a difficult marriage, you can run from a tough job, you can run from a difficulty—but you will eventually end up there again. The trouble is in you, and you can't run away from yourself any more than you can run away from God: ask Jonah.

Overcoming Adversity

In Acts 16, when Paul and Silas find themselves in prison, they take a wonderful approach to their adversity. *About midnight Paul and Silas were praying and singing hymns to God* (v. 25). Having been jailed for proclaiming the gospel in the streets and marketplace, they see prison through the eyes of faith, as merely a change of venue, and continued their witness.

I don't know the last time I rejoiced in the midst of my difficulty. It's a lot easier to rejoice after the trial is over. Why didn't they wait and rejoice and sing hymns after they got out of prison? That would have made more sense. However, they had so much faith that God was going to see them through that they could praise Him *in advance* for His deliverance.

Prison wasn't Paul's only difficulty. He wrote in 2 Corinthians 11:24–25, *"Five times I received from the Jews the forty lashes minus one. Three times I was beaten with rods, once I was stoned, three times I was shipwrecked."* Yet he still found strength to glorify God, whatever his earthly situation!

Have you ever heard someone say, "Oh, you wouldn't have any problems if you just walked more closely with God. If you had more faith, all your needs would be met." Well, if you truly had that expectation—that something lacking in your own efforts kept God from working miracles in your life—you wouldn't be a mature Christian either, because God intentionally allows us those problems. Paul said, *"If I must boast, I will boast of the things that show my weakness"* (2 Co 11:30). Our weakness shows God's power.

Later Paul also wrote: *Therefore I will boast all the more gladly about my weaknesses, so that Christ's power may rest on me. That is why, for Christ's sake, I delight in weaknesses, in insults, in hardships, in persecutions, in difficulties. For when I am weak, then I am strong* (2 Co 12:9–10). What an amazing testimony!

When you have difficulties, thank God for bringing them into your life. Your infirmity or difficulty will become His blessing on your life.

Like Paul, we need to face our difficulties.

With faith, not doubt.

With hope, not despair. God will meet you at your level of dependency and expectancy. Don't give up!

With joy, not happiness. Happiness is a flimsy emotion. True joy, true rejoicing, can only come in response to adversity. No circumstance should be allowed to steal your joy. It is your choice.

With perseverance, not surrender. Keep standing. Keep praying. Keep believing. Keep hoping. It will take courage and determination, which God will provide through the Holy Spirit.

With peace, not worry. See your life as God sees it. Even if you think it's falling to pieces, it's not when God is in control. *The peace of God, which transcends all understanding, will guard your heart and your minds* (Ph 4:7).

With deliverance, not bondage. Do you live in expectation of His deliverance, or do you wallow in your bondage? You don't have to allow your condition to determine how you see yourself. We are not created to live in defeat. *No, in all these things we are more than conquerors through him who loved us* (Ro 8:37).

As a victor, not a victim. Too many of us are whiners. God has destined us to live in victory, but we have to do our part by having the attitude of a victor.

With strength, not weakness. God wants to exchange our strength for His sufficiency. Our strength doesn't come from ourselves, but from God giving us His strength in place of our weakness.

Knowing we may be down, but we're not out. You may be down on the outside, but you needn't be down on the inside. You may be financially broke, you may be emotionally broke, you may be unemployed; but inside you can stand up, saying, "I'm not going to let this circumstance, this difficulty, this adversity take me down on the inside. God sees the big picture, and He is working to conform my character to greater Christ-likeness."

As winners, not whiners. The power to propel us to our potential is found in our response to our adversities and to our difficulties. Whether we become winners is not what this lifetime is about. It's about our eternal destiny. The journey and the process will lead us to the point where we stand before God and hear Him say, "Well done, my good and faithful servant."

God Uses Our Adversity

In 2 Corinthians 4:7–9, Paul wrote:

> *We have this treasure in jars of clay to show that this all-surpassing power is from God and not from us. We are hard pressed on every side but not crushed; perplexed, but not in despair; persecuted, but not abandoned; struck down, but not destroyed.*

Another wonderful passage to remember in adversity is Romans 5:1–5:

> *Therefore, since we have been justified through faith, we have peace with God through our Lord Jesus Christ, through whom we have gained access by faith into this grace in which we now stand. And we rejoice in hope of the glory of God. Not only so, but we also **rejoice in our sufferings,** because we know that suffering produces perseverance; perseverance, character; and character, hope. And hope does not disappoint us, because God has poured out his love into our hearts by the Holy Spirit, whom he has given us.*

(author's emphasis)

What God wants to do within us is created out of our tribulations. He uses adversity:

- To chisel out what does not belong there.
- To propel us to His "Greater Yes!"
- As steps to our potential.
- To move us toward our destiny.

When I lived in the country, one of my favorite farmers was George Silva. He taught me a lot of lessons from the fields and acres. One day he asked me to jump in his truck and go for a ride. We drove to a large field where he was growing silage corn. It looked wilted. I asked him, "What is wrong with your corn?"

He said to me, "I have to let it get under stress. This way when I do shoot water to it, the corn will grow a foot a day. Then I will do it again. This corn will grow sixteen to twenty feet tall. You can actually hear the corn grow."

Then he took me to a low part of the field where the water drained and settled. The corn there was stunted. He said, "See, this is what happens when you get too much of a good thing." Believe it or not, we should thank God for adversities and difficulties.

Remember, God sees and knows the "big picture." He knows what He needs to put in your life to propel you to your "Greater Yes!" So the question is: How are you facing your difficulties? Are you running from them? Are you hiding from them? They are the things God is using in your life to conform you to the image of Christ. God cannot develop your "Greater Yes!" without adversities and difficulties

Imagine the possibilities!

MOVING TOWARD MY "GREATER YES!"

1. What adversities and difficulties is God allowing in my life?

2. Why is God allowing these adversities and difficulties in my life?

3. How do I see my adversities and difficulties?

4. How am I facing my adversities and difficulties?

5. What have I learned that will help me move toward my "Greater Yes!"?

MY PRAYER OF COMMITMENT

Father, thank You for adversities and difficulties. I realize that You use them in my life to propel me to my "Greater Yes!" I will not allow ___(Example: My divorce)___ to control my potential and my destiny. I am looking forward to what You're going to do in and through me. Chisel the image of Your Son in me and give me the courage to press on and not give up. For when I am weak, then I am made strong. Amen.

⮞ Chapter 21 ⮜

Get Plugged In

God wants you plugging into the power that is already within you.

Prayer is the most powerful tool Christians have. The "Greater Yes!" is not about self-discipline or self-control. Prayer is about plugging into the power of the Spirit that lives within every believer. I have wondered what life would be like if I would submit my life continually to the power of the Spirit. As a believer, I know I do not need more of the Holy Spirit. He needs more of me.

Holy Spirit + Your Prayers = God's Power Released

In Matthew 6, Jesus Christ taught his disciples how to pray using what we now call The Lord's Prayer. The context of this passage begins at Jesus' baptism, where God said, *"This is my Son, whom I love; with him I am well pleased"* (Ma 3:17). Immediately after that, God led him into the desert (see Ma 4). Did you know that when God is pleased with you, He leads you into the desert to be tempted by the devil?

Jesus came out of the desert and began to call His disciples, teaching them among other things the incredible principles of Matthew 5–7: the Sermon on the Mount. In Matthew 6, verses 7–8 he says, *"When you pray, do not keep on babbling like pagans, for they think they will be heard because of their many words. Do not be like them, for your Father knows what you need before you ask him."*

Why pray if God already knows? Because prayer is not for Him—it is for us. God never says, "Oops. I didn't know she would ask for that." Prayer brings our will in line with God's. Jesus then told His disciples,

"This, then, is how you should pray: Our Father in heaven, hal-
lowed be your name, your kingdom come, your will be done on earth
as it is in heaven. Give us today our daily bread. Forgive us our
debts, as we also have forgiven our debtors. And lead us not into
temptation, but deliver us from the evil one."

Mark 6:9 13

I have to say it again: behind every problem, there is an unmet
need. We spend a great deal of our time focusing on the problem,
beating up the problem, discussing the problem, trying to bring answers to the problem—yet the problem is often only a symptom, a be-
havioral or physical manifestation of a deeper, unmet need.

God gives us solutions to those needs in this prayer. There are many
prayers in scripture, but in this particular prayer many of the basic needs
we have in life are answered. Why do we work so hard, worry so much,
and believe so little for our needs? When all else fails, then we pray.

Sometimes I get up in the morning and jump on the roller coaster
of life, giving it all my effort to make sure it stays on the track. While
I'm hanging on for dear life, God is smiling at me. "Why are you doing this? Why don't you just look to me and let go?"

We have seven basic power needs, all of which are addressed in the
Lord's Prayer. As we look at these together, remember that behind
every problem is an unmet need.

Your Problems + What You See = Unmet Needs

Inferiority

At some point, everyone—young and old, men and women—struggles with an improper self-image because Satan has tried to persuade
us that we are not God's best, that we are junk.

The unmet need behind the problem of inferiority is our identity
and significance. God's answer is His presence: *Our Father in heaven,*
hallowed be your name. Our identity is not in what we can earn or how
we look in the mirror; it is in what God says about us.

Why does God love us? Because we are His. We have a daddy. The
Aramaic word translated "Father" in our New Testament is *Abba*,
which signifies an intimate relationship. When you feel lonely and
you've messed up, God says, "Come crawl up in my lap. I'll hold you
and tell you the truth about who you are." It's not what this world says
about you, but what God says that *is* important.

Confusion

Do you ever feel confused and frustrated, wondering where you're going next? Do you ask yourself, "What is God's will for my life?" If you will believe in true faith that He will lead you and take care of you, you won't be wondering where you're going next! I was confused and frustrated when I was nineteen years old. There are a lot of people living in total confusion, who are living on a roller coaster and don't know what's coming up in the next tunnel.

The unmet need behind our confusion is a need for direction. The answer is God's plan and purpose: *Your kingdom come, Your will be done on earth as it is in heaven.* God's will shall prevail on earth—that is a guarantee. Do you want direction? Ask God; He has already answered you in scripture. *"I know the plans I have for you," declares the* LORD, *"plans to prosper you and not to harm you, plans to give you hope and a future"* (Je 29:11). Our purpose in life is to serve God by serving His church and His people.

If somebody offered me a job with a million-dollar salary, starting tomorrow, I would say, "No, that's not what God called me to do. That's not His purpose for my life." If you want direction, do what Jesus did. He followed the will of His Father.

We know who's in control of the roller coaster because He made it. When I get on a theme park roller coaster, I don't usually know the builder. But life is one roller coaster I can get on with confidence because I know who is keeping it on track, and I know His will is going to be done.

Worry

My definition of worry is concern out of control. God wants to turn your worry into worship. I like to raise my hands in surrender to God—kind of like those guys on the roller coaster who wave their arms over their heads and shout, "Woohoo!" I am excited about what God is doing, because I know who is in control.

The unmet need of our worry is a need to worshipfully trust God as our provider, as in: g*ive us today our daily bread.* Although you may think you are the provider in your home, or that your spouse is, it is actually God who is the ultimate provider. Jesus said, *"I tell you, do not worry about your life"* (Ma 6:25). How do we do that? By understanding God is the provider.

Paul wrote*: Do not be anxious about anything, but in everything, by* *prayer and petition, with thanksgiving, present your requests to God. And the peace of God, which transcends all understanding, will guard your hearts and your minds in Christ Jesus* (Ph 4:6–7). We do not have to be anxious about anything. God's all-surpassing peace guards us from worry.

Guilt

When you feel guilty as a believer, you need to look Satan in the eye and say: *There is now no condemnation for those who are in Christ Jesus* (Ro 8:1). Should we feel conviction? Yes. But we don't have to feel guilty. Satan likes to make us feel guilty so we won't feel that we're accepted.

Behind the problem of our guilt is the unmet need for acceptance. God's pardon is the answer as we pray: *forgive us our debts*. God accepts us as we are, but he loves us too much to keep us the way we are.

Guilt and condemnation are not from God. To understand our true position, we need to listen to the Holy Spirit and accept God's forgiveness.

Relationships

In all the counseling I've done, every relationship issue has come down to a need for forgiveness. To forgive is to release. In order to release God's power in your life, you have to be able to forgive.

At the end of the prayer, Jesus jumped right into this issue. *"If you forgive men when they sin against you, your heavenly Father will also forgive you. But if you do not forgive men their sins, your Father will not forgive your sins"* (Ma 6:14–15). In a sense, he was saying, "I won't even hear your prayer as long as you hold a grudge against someone else."

The answer to our relational needs is God's power of forgiveness. As long as we won't forgive, we put ourselves in bondage and God will not forgive us. That's the only thing in scripture that God says he cannot do—he cannot forgive you if you are not willing to forgive another (Ma 6:15).

God offers you the power to forgive, the ability to forgive our debtors. Jesus also said that if you are at the altar with your offering and remember that you needed to restore your relationship with your brother, you should go take care of that first (Ma 5:23–24). Your worship to God is empty unless you're willing to go forgive that person in your life.

Temptation

Scripture never says, "Pray about your temptation." It says, "Flee from it." 1 Corinthians 10:13 says: *No temptation has seized you except what is common to man. And God is faithful; he will not let you be tempted beyond what you can bear. But when you are tempted, he will also provide a way out so that you can stand up under it.*

I had a friend who committed adultery with a co-worker. They were both believers. I asked him, "What went wrong?" He said they were praying about their temptation instead of fleeing from it.

There is not one temptation that God allows in your life that does not come with a way of escape. When we pray: *lead us not into temptation*, God's answer is His protection, the way out. Every time I'm tempted, I'm stepping outside of the authority of God's word. My real need is for protection. Satan will lie and say God can't cover you. Don't listen to him. Stay under the cover of your Heavenly Father, and you will always see the way out of temptation.

Fears

Our real need is not actually a matter of fear; it's a matter of trust. We need someone to trust, so we pray: *Deliver us from the evil one.* Just reading the newspaper or watching the news can make us fearful about the world we live in. The bottom line is: Whom do I trust?

God's answer to our need for trust is His peace. When I'm trying to control life and keep it on track, as I start going up a hill, I get fearful about what's on the other side. But God says, "No, let go. Trust me. I'm the Creator. Don't trust what you see around you. Trust in me, and I will take care of you."

I don't have to fear, because I've ridden this roller coaster long enough to know God isn't going to let me get off the track. God knows the day I'm appointed to go to heaven. No enemy can determine my future. I don't know the future, but I know who holds the future, and I know whom I trust.

I once read about a guy who lived in so much fear that he wrapped his house in duct tape and plastic. He began to suffocate. I'm pretty sure he did not know Jesus, because if he did, he would know that nothing we do will change God's determined will. We can have peace knowing everything that happens to us is in His plan.

What or whom are you looking to for the solutions to your most personal needs? Are you focused on the problem or on the solution?

We all have problems of inferiority, confusion, worry, guilt, relationships, temptations, or fears, but I want you to know we have a solution in God's presence, in His person, His plan, and His purpose, His provision, His power, His protection, and His peace. It's all in this prayer.

> If you can say, *"Our Father in heaven"*—you are in personal, intimate relationship with your Heavenly Father.
>
> If you can say, *"Hallowed be Your name"*—Christ is first in your life and you are following His direction.
>
> If you can say, *"Your will be done on earth"*—you are committed to doing God's will above your own.
>
> If you can say, *"Give us today our daily bread"*—you are turning your worry into worship.
>
> If you can say, *"Forgive us our debts"*—you have accepted God's redemption and are being set free.
>
> If you can say, *"As we also have forgiven our debtors"*—you have the power to forgive and set others free.
>
> If you can say, *"And lead us not into temptation"*—you are exercising God's personal protection.
>
> If you can say, *"But deliver us from the evil one"*—you trust your Father and peace rules in your heart and life.

Prayer is the next best thing to being with God himself. Jabez got plugged in when he prayed: *Oh, that you would bless me and enlarge my territory! Let your hand be with me and keep me from harm so that I will be free from pain* (1 Ch 4:10). And God granted his request.

When my daughter was seven months pregnant, we were discussing her future. She said she was not sure if any man would ever love her. God gave me an incredible insight. He told me to tell her that God never says, "Oops." God already knew what she needed better than we did. So we prayed and God answered. Three years later, she met the love of her life, he adopted her daughter, and they now have three other children.

God is asking us to:

P.U.S.H.—Pray Until Something Happens—
Imagine the possibilities!

MOVING TOWARD MY "GREATER YES!"

1. To what or whom am I looking to empower my life?

2. Do I feel my life is out of control?

3. What am I doing to "plug in" to the Holy Spirit?

4. What is keeping me from "plugging in"?

5. What have I learned that will help me move toward my "Greater Yes!"?

MY PRAYER OF COMMITMENT

Our Father in heaven, hallowed be Your name, Your kingdom come, Your will be done on earth as it is in heaven. Give us today our daily bread. Forgive us our debts, as we also have forgiven our debtors. And lead us not into temptation, but deliver us from the evil one. For Yours is the kingdom and the glory and the power forever and ever. Amen.

SECTION 4

Deploying Your "Greater Yes!"

It is time to do something about finding your "Greater Yes!" It is not enough to say you want a life that echoes in eternity. You have to do something about it. There are seven factors you need to realize when deploying your "Greater Yes!"

- You will become who you soar with—addresses your altitude!

- You have to forget what lies behind—addresses your past!

- You have to descend to find true greatness—addresses your attitude!

- You have to give yourself away—addresses your blessing!

- You have to mark where God is moving—addresses your impact!

- You have to never give up—addresses your persistence!

- You have to realize it is about how you end the race, not how you start it—addresses your finish!

Live your life so loudly that others want to hear your words!

❧ CHAPTER 22 ❧

Soaring with Eagles

You will become whom you soar with!

I've read that two sources of energy keep eagles soaring. One is the energy from upward-moving air that provides lift. The other is energy from the sun. Uneven heating of the air just above the ground causes the formation of "thermals," which serve as air escalators. Once the eagles have attained sufficient height, they swoop out and down, relying on the momentum of their decent to propel them into flight.[1]

Discovering our "Greater Yes!" involves a clear understanding of who we are—our value—whose we are, why we were created, and what we're destined to become. I believe we are created to be soaring eagles, yet many of us spend our lives pecking with the turkeys.

I define eagles as those who are looking up, seeking to soar toward their God-given destiny to live a life that echoes in eternity. Turkeys are those who are looking down, pecking in the dust of earthly things with no thought of eternity.

Are you an eagle or a turkey? Sadly, many Christians have been told that only a chosen few can be eagles, but the rest of us have to be turkeys, so we might as well peck at life, because we won't become anything more. But that's not what God has called us to do. He wants us to soar, to live the new life by new principles, passions, purposes, and potential for now and for eternity.

Are you soaring or are you grounded? Are you using your wings like the lofty eagle, or are you just flapping at life like the earth-bound turkey? Are you just blending in with other turkeys, comfortably basting in your lukewarm faith, content with just enough of God to get to heaven? If so, it's time to look up and get a better view of God and His call on your life to soar like an eagle.

Waiting + God = Mounting UP!

Here's what the prophet Isaiah said:

"To whom will you compare me? Or who is my equal?" says the Holy One. Lift your eyes and look to the heavens: Who created all these? He who brings out the starry host one by one, and calls them each by name. Because of his great power and mighty strength, not one of them is missing. Do you not know? Have you not heard? The LORD is the everlasting God, the Creator of the ends of the earth. He will not grow tired or weary, and his understanding no one can fathom. He gives strength to the weary and increases the power of the weak. Even youths grow tired and weary, and young men stumble and fall; but those who hope in the LORD will renew their strength. They will soar on wings like eagles; they will run and not grow weary, they will walk and not be faint.
Isaiah 40:25–26, 28–31

What Keeps Us Soaring?

A pilot friend of mine flies stealth bombers. One day I asked him how he kept his plane in the air. He explained to me that basically four things determine if the plane will fly: attitude, altitude, airspeed, and aptitude. As I thought about these, I realized that the principles that keep an airplane in the air are the same principles that keep us soaring in life.

It takes attitude. The position of the plane in relation to the horizon—whether the nose is up or down—is the attitude indicator. That speaks to our mind and our thinking. Many of us live like turkeys, with our beaks down. God says, "Lift up your eyes to heaven. Keep your nose up, like an eagle." Attitude is the perspective of a man in relationship to God.

It takes altitude. The height of the plane in relation to the earth's surface is its altitude. That speaks to our heart. What we are feeling? What dimension do we live in? How do we see our world? We were never meant to just exist. Altitude is the heart of a man in relationship to the world.

It takes airspeed. The speed of the plane in relation to its performance is the airspeed. This speaks to our soul. The problem is that a lot of us don't move; we get stuck. Moving targets are harder to hit, but when we're immobilized Satan starts taking us out. Airspeed is the will of a man in relationship to himself. God says, "Are you willing to obey me? Do you really want to reach your potential and destiny?"

It takes aptitude. The capacity of the plane in relation to its potential is aptitude. It speaks to our strength. Where do you find your power? We try to do everything in our own strength, instead of plugging in and saying, "God, I need your power." Life can't be just about us; otherwise, we'll never soar. We'll end up flapping our wings two feet above ground. Eagles know where the wind currents are; they know where the power is. The power of the Holy Spirit is going to keep us going. Aptitude is the potential of a man in relationship to his destiny.

Attitude + Altitude + Airspeed + Aptitude = Soaring

When we love God with all our heart, mind, soul, and strength, we will keep soaring. Otherwise, we will remain grounded (Ma 22:37–39).

What Keeps Us Grounded?

Stinking thinking means our attitude is nose down. What is going through your head? Are fear, doubt, frustration, and self-dependency in there? That will keep you grounded. God wants to elevate your attitude, first by transforming your thinking. Proper thinking leads to proper speaking, which leads to proper feelings, which leads to proper living, which leads you to your potential.

A hard heart means our altitude is too low. Disobedience, a lost relationship, lack of forgiveness, lack of prayer, and neglect of being in the Word are things that ground us. We can all have a hard heart at times. Maybe we need to adjust our altitude and confess those things that are keeping us grounded so we can soar.

A closed spirit means our airspeed is too low. Do you have an open spirit? Or have you allowed life and circumstances to quench your spirit? Are you angry or are you withdrawing and escaping? Are you fighting or just resentful? Those are the evidences of a closed spirit. What kind of spirit do you carry into your business? What kind of spirit do you carry into your home?

False success means our aptitude is weak. This is evidenced by self-centeredness, stress, and valuing things more than people. If we seek success and fulfillment in things that don't really matter for eternity, we are being turkeys. God wants to use our gifts, multiply our resources, and maximize our opportunities. He wants us to be successful in the things that really matter, such as marriage, family, spiritual walk, and our "Greater Yes!" Where do you spend your time, your talent, your treasure, and your touch? That's where your priority is, and that's where your success is. God doesn't offer you temporary success. He offers you eternal significance.

Who Are You Flying With?

What kind of people do you hang with? Who brings you up and who brings you down? Whether you're grounded or whether you're soaring with eagles, the company you keep will have a tremendous impact on whether you stay caged or continue to soar as God intended.

Turkeys bring us down; eagles mount us up. If we truly love our Christian brothers and sisters, we're going to help them mount up and soar. Coddling their pain and weakness will only keep them pecking with the turkeys. Think about the people you spend the most time with: your boss, your employees, your spouse, your children, and your friends. Do they encourage you to live up to your potential? Do you encourage them?

Turkeys tear us down; eagles build us up. Building up another person doesn't mean you always agree with everything he or she says. Sometimes it might mean saying, "Hey, I see sin in your life. You've got to stop that." My wife is the most important eagle I soar with. She watches out for me and tells me when I'm not having the right attitude, altitude, airspeed, or aptitude. I would rather have eagles building me up and helping me, even by correcting me, than turkeys sitting around and keeping me pecking at meaningless stuff.

Turkeys don't want us to stand out; eagles push us out of our comfort zone (nest). Turkeys will tell us, "Just be kind, be a good Christian, and you'll go to heaven, and everything will be great." Eagles will keep encouraging us to get out there and make a difference instead of just settling into our comfortable nest.

Turkeys encourage us to succeed at what doesn't matter; eagles encourage us to find significance in what really matters. Eagles have a "Greater Yes!" We need to be hanging around people who are also concerned with living a life that echoes in eternity. Our closest friends should be those who won't let us stay on our map and dwell in our past. They should encourage us to succeed at what really matters.

Turkeys keep us "stuck in neutral;" eagles propel us to our potential. Some of us get settled into our nests of mediocrity. Turkeys don't travel far. We are meant to be eagles that soar high above the earth for miles in the distance and realize our potential.

Who are you soaring with? You will become whom you soar with. Are you in a small group with other believers? If you are a broken-winged eagle, you especially need a group of healed eagles around you.

It is said that two sources of energy keep us soaring. One is the energy from the Holy Spirit within us that provides our power. The other is the energy we draw from a personal intimate relationship with the Son, Jesus Christ. God wants us to soar at higher levels of faith and dependence. Once we have attained sufficient trust we can soar to our "Greater Yes!" Remember, we become who or what we soar with. Mount up with wings as eagles.

Imagine the possibilities!

MOVING TOWARD MY "GREATER YES!"

1. Am I soaring or grounded?

2. What is keeping me soaring? Keeping me grounded?

3. Who are the turkeys and eagles in my life?

4. How can I be an eagle to others?

5. What have I learned that will help me move toward my "Greater Yes!"?

MY PRAYER OF COMMITMENT

Lord, I know I have spent some time pecking with the turkeys. Now I am ready to live up to my potential and find wings to soar like an eagle. Please help me find others who can encourage me and whom I can encourage to discover, develop, and deploy our "Greater Yes!" Amen.

~ CHAPTER 23 ~

Letting Go of the Past

You have to forget what lies behind.

We will never reach our "Greater Yes!" if we are not willing to let go of the past. You can take hold of the destiny God has for you because your past does not have to determine your future or your potential. But you will never be able to grab hold of the future until you let go of the past.

God loves to use people who are "do-overs," anyone who has been offered and accepted a fresh start. We all qualify.

Paul wrote, *Now we look inside, and what we see is that anyone united with the Messiah gets a **fresh start**, is created anew. The old life is gone; a new life burgeons!* (2 Co 5:17 MSG, author's emphasis).

Your Letting Go + God = Your Potential!

Out of sheer generosity he put us in right standing with himself. A pure gift. He got us out of the mess we're in and restored us to where he always wanted us to be. And he did it by means of Jesus Christ" (Ro 3:24 MSG).

There is a direct relationship between the pain of the past and our present level of intimacy with God and others. The more we live in the past, the less intimacy we have in the present.

In his book *Your Best Life Now*, Joel Osteen wrote,

> *You dare not use your past as an excuse for your current bad attitude or as a rationalization for your unwillingness to forgive somebody...Don't hold on to feelings of bitterness and resentment and let them poison your future. Let go of those hurts and pains. Forgive the people who did you wrong. Forgive yourself for the mistakes you made.*[1]

In the first part of this book, we considered the life of the crippled man in John 5. He was stuck on his mat, unable to move toward his potential. Jesus Christ asked him that unusual question: *"Do you want to get well?"* (Jo 5:6). It appears on the face of it a strange question because who wouldn't want to get well? But Jesus saw that the man had become comfortable with his disease. After all, he had been lying there for thirty-eight years.

Sometimes our past becomes our comfort zone. I've heard that people in prison feel very claustrophobic in their prison cells for the first year or two, but then they get kind of used to it. After twenty years they feel exposed without the prison bars.

The invalid man told Jesus, "There's no one to put me into the pool." Our pain becomes an excuse for our present decisions, defaulting to a Lesser Yes. You can't change the past, but if it is a burden to you, a source of guilt and shame that prevents you from developing your God-given potential, let me share some good news with you: it is possible to lay that burden down. You need to decide whether you are going to sit around by the pool of self-pity for thirty-eight years like the crippled man at the well or get up and move on with your life.

Hebrews 12:1 says, *Let us throw off everything that hinders and the sin that so easily entangles, and let us run with perseverance the race marked out for us.* We have to let go of everything that's tripping us up and weighing us down.

The past should serve as a point of reference, not a place of residence. When we are trapped in the past, the past is always present, and it seeks to define who and whose we are. When we allow the past to define us, our own failures, our wounds, our past, our debt, our addiction all become part of the present, and they limit our potential.

Some signs that you may be trapped in the past are bitterness, self-pity, unforgiveness, addiction, disappointment, anger, blame, guilt, or hurt. I personally struggle with fear of failure and my lack of trust. I drove myself to succeed, and spent eleven years in seminary to prove wrong a college professor who said I would never make it. When my wife and I started People Matter Ministries, I was afraid because I didn't want to raise support and have to trust other people's gifts for my income. I didn't want to depend on anybody, only my own work and abilities.

It took me awhile to overcome my fear of failure and fear of other people letting me down. But God showed me it was tripping me up from running the race He has called me to. I am understanding more and more what Paul meant when he wrote, *Forgetting what is behind and straining toward what is ahead, I press on toward the goal to win the prize for which God has called me heavenward in Christ Jesus* (Ph 3:13–14).

Freeing Ourselves from the Past

God doesn't take a bad thing away from us without giving us something good to fill the vacuum. When he breaks you free from an addiction or from a painful past, he gives you a "Greater Yes!" to take their place. God does not leave you empty. Ask Him to take off anger, and He's going to put on joy; ask him to cool down hatred, and He'll set you afire with love. First, as with Peter starting to walk on the sea toward Jesus, we have to step out of our boat. You need to **rise out of your emotional bondage and pick up freedom.** Jesus gave the invalid man the opportunity to take up his mat and experience freedom. Our emotional bondage, our bitterness and anger, can be replaced by Christ's freedom.

Rise out of your mental bondage and take up peace. God wants you to walk away from self-pity and self-loathing and enter into His peace.

Rise out of your relational bondage and into forgiveness. That doesn't mean God wants you to leave your wife. Instead, he wants you to quit the blame and resentment, and remove the bondage from your relationships by setting yourself and other people free with forgiveness.

Rise out of your spiritual bondage and take up power. We don't have to live in guilt and condemnation. God wants to set us free to have a relationship with Him.

Rise out of your physical bondage and into redemption. We don't have to practice sin anymore. If an alcoholic gives up drinking without finding redemption, he just becomes a dry drunk. Even though he may not be drinking, he still has the same anger and issues he faced when he was drinking. As long as you're hanging onto the pain of the past, even if you've broken the need and practice of addiction, you'll still have the anger, bitterness, resentment, and pain that drove you to the addiction in the first place.

Rise out of your situational bondage and into victory. I must not let my circumstances dictate who I am, how angry I will be, or whether I feel like a failure. God wants to give us victory and power rise above our circumstances. There will be disappointments and defeats, but we won't be defined by them. We'll be defined by what God says about us.

Rise out of the bondage of missed and bungled opportunities—lost potential—and take up your "Greater Yes!" God wants to fill us with not just any potential, but *His* potential. He will take us places we never imagined and bring us to a greater level of intimacy.

Grace + Forgiveness = Freedom

How Do I Break Free?

The apostle Paul wrote: *What a wretched man I am! Who will rescue me from this body of death?* (Ro 7:24). In the Old Testament, when a man killed someone, the law required that the dead body be tied to him, and he would have to carry it around. That's how Paul felt about his sin—it was weighing him down. Do you feel that way at times?

God told Paul, *"My grace is sufficient for you"* (2 Co 12:9). No matter what you are dragging around with you, no matter what in your past has a hold on you, God's grace is sufficient. Later, Paul was able to write: *Not that I have already obtained all this, or have already been made perfect, but I press on to take hold of that which for Christ Jesus took hold of me* (Ph 3:12).

As long as you're hanging onto the past, you can't grab your potential. Wherever I am, I'm going to press forward to the call of my Lord. With the strength found in the Holy Spirit, I have to forget—or if not forget, at least forgive and stop dwelling on—what lies behind so I can press on to what lies ahead.

Letting Go

What are the steps to letting go of the past?

1. Consider what or who is keeping you from letting go of your past, thus blocking your potential. What can't you let go of? Are you, like the crippled man on his mat, depending on some unknown hero to put you in that pool? Isn't that just an excuse?
2. Confess to yourself and to God what you're dealing with. Say, "God, I do fear, I do lack faith; I'm afraid I'm going to fail. Forgive the iniquity of my sins, and give me the strength to stop beating myself up because of my past."

3. Then you have to release the past to God. Let go of it and give it to God. On Calvary's cross Jesus took the sins of the world upon Himself and paid the just price for them, in our place. Do you think Christ has stopped taking away the guilt for your failures? For Jesus' sake, God wants you to leave your past back where it belongs and let Him change your ways—it's called repentance. Once you have truly done that, he will give you the power to go on.

4. Trust God to bring justice into your life. He will take your wrong and make it right. Remember, vengeance is the Lord's.

5. Take the steps necessary to bring healing from the past hurts and wounds. We all have some wounds in our lives that need to be dealt with before we can really move on. There may be someone you need to forgive or someone from whom you need to seek forgiveness.

6. Find your "Greater Yes!" so you can move forward. I encourage you to work through the chapters at the end of this book, which will help you discover your unique "Greater Yes!" If you do not fill that vacuum with God's "Greater Yes!", you will fill it up with the world's lesser yeses.

7. Press on and take hold of your God-given potential and destiny.

Everything we need for our "Greater Yes!" is found in a deep, intimate relationship with God. Everything in our future, everything in our potential, everything in our legacy, everything in our destiny is found in Him. We don't have to rely on the pool of outward circumstances anymore; we can get up and walk. Your past does not have to define or determine your potential or destiny. God will use your past to propel and compel you to your "Greater Yes!"

Imagine the possibilities!

Moving Toward My "Greater Yes!"

1. What am I hanging on to that will keep me from my "Greater Yes!"?

2. What evidences are there in my life that I am trapped in the past?

3. What must I do to be free from my past?

4. What is God asking me to break free to?

5. What have I learned that will help me move toward my "Greater Yes!"?

MY PRAYER OF COMMITMENT

Father, thank You for my past. I now release to You my past and set myself on a course to my "Greater Yes!" I will not allow _____ to control my potential and my destiny. I am looking forward to what You are going to do in and through me. Give me the courage, Father, to let go and press on to Your call through my relationship with Jesus Christ. Amen.

~ CHAPTER 24 ~

A Greatness that Descends

You have to descend to find true greatness.

We were in the middle of a Sunday evening service when a drunk stumbled into the church. Dad was leading worship. The man staggered all the way down the aisle until he literally fell on his knees at the altar.

My dad immediately turned the service over to my mom, walked across to the desperate man, and knelt down beside him. As my dad put his arm around the man and prayed for him, the man began to weep. As my dad entered into his pain, despair, and suffering, he was able to lead the man to Jesus Christ that night.

From where I sat observing, I saw only a smelly, nasty drunk. But my dad saw a man without a shepherd, felt compassion for him, and entered into his pain (Mk 6:34).

Your Love + Your Humility + Your Service = True Greatness

Looking back, I now know what I saw at that altar years ago: greatness descending. You will never be as great as when you are descending. If we are going to become truly great in our "Greater Yes!" we have to have a greatness that is willing to descend, an attitude of humility.

Paul wrote to the Philippians about the attitude of true greatness. *Your attitude should be the same as that of Christ Jesus: Who, being in very nature God, did not consider equality with God something to be grasped, but made himself nothing, taking the very nature of a servant, being made in human likeness* (Ph 2:5–7).

The kind of greatness that Christ—and my dad that day—demonstrated was countercultural. Descending is normally reserved for losers, cowards, failures, and the weak. Our society tells us to avoid this at all costs. In a meeting, the one who doesn't say anything, the one who does not have all the answers, is considered a loser. People say, "He just doesn't have the leadership skills." It's the loud guy who often gets promoted.

Ascending is reserved for winners, heroes, the successful, the strong, and the proud. The world says advancing higher is to be admired and pursued. You ascend to fame, money, glory, power, comfort, and pleasure. Up is the direction of greatness. Humility is weak. Do whatever it takes to conquer gravity.

This is a lie! Jesus never discarded people who desired to be great or to do great things, but he did redefine what true greatness is, what it means, and how to achieve it.

The Paradox

There is a contradiction between the culture's view and God's view. The culture says, rise to the highest level of your company, make movies, be a talented athlete, rake in a lot of money, accumulate all the tools and succeed at what does not matter, and you will be called great. The only direction is up!

God's view is a paradox: True greatness is not a measure of self-will or self-achievement but rather self-abandonment. The more you are willing to give up, the more you gain, in Christ. Succeed at what really matters, and you will live great. The only direction is down!

Discussion at a business meeting was not going well, so I was getting ready to stand up and give them a piece of my mind. God said to me, "Who do you think you are?" I literally had to get out of my chair and go down on my knees so I wouldn't rise up, because I would have been out of the will of God. It doesn't matter how right you are. Whenever you think you've got to rise up, go down.

Jesus was dealing with this paradox of greatness with his own disciples. The disciples were convinced that Christ came to establish an earthly kingdom. They had just experienced the triumphal entry of the Messiah into Jerusalem and were expecting Him to overthrow the Roman authority and set up an earthly, political kingdom.

The disciples got caught up in all the glory and praise. The mother of James and John put a good word in for her two sons, which stirred up some dissension in the disciple's ranks. She requested of Jesus, *"Grant that one of these two sons of mine may sit at your right and the other at your left in your kingdom"* (Ma 20:21).

If they had ears to hear, the disciples would have realized they were fighting over something that was not Christ's to give. It is the Father who gives true greatness.

Just before the Last Supper, Jesus demonstrated true love, humility, and servanthood to His disciples by washing their feet. He closed with this statement:

> *"You call me 'Teacher' and 'Lord,' and rightly so, for that is what I am. Now that I, your Lord and Teacher, have washed your feet, you also should wash one another's feet. I have set you an example that you should do as I have done for you. I tell you the truth, no servant is greater than his master, nor is a messenger greater than the one who sent him. Now that you know these things, you will be* **blessed** *if you do them."*
>
> John 13:13–17 (author's emphasis)

Luke's gospel states that thusly:

> *Within minutes* [after the washing of the feet and the Lord's Supper] *they* [disciples] *were bickering over who of them would end up the greatest. But Jesus intervened: "Kings like to throw their weight around and people in authority like to give themselves fancy titles. It's not going to be that way with you. Let the senior among you become like the junior; let the leader act the part of a servant."*
>
> Luke 22:24–26 MSG

This demonstration by Jesus was not just about washing feet. It was about love, humility, and service.

Christ Descended into Greatness Because He Knew

It is clear from John 13 that Jesus could descend and become a servant even to the point of dying on a cross because He knew:

Who He was—which speaks to His identity. He knew His Father had put Him in complete charge of everything (v. 1).

Whose He was—which speaks to His significance. He knew He had come from God and was returning to God (v. 1).

Why He was created—which speaks to His purpose. He knew He had come to die on a cross (Ph 2:8).

What He was destined to become—which speaks to His potential and destiny. He knew God would exalt Him to the highest place and give Him a name above every name, and at His name every knee will

bow in heaven and on earth and under the earth, and every tongue
will confess Him as Lord, to the glory of God the Father (Ph 2:9–11).

We Can Descend Into Greatness Because We Know...

Why can we descend into greatness? Because of what we know: *For we
are God's workmanship, created in Christ Jesus to do good works, which
God prepared in advance for us to do* (Ep 2:10).

Who I am—which speaks to our identity. Because we are chosen
and marked by God's love, and because He delights in us (Ma 3:17),
we are His workmanship and masterpiece.

Whose we are—which speaks to our significance. We are God's
adopted sons and daughters and will spend eternity with Him in
heaven because we were created in Christ Jesus.

Why we were created—which speaks to our purpose. We are new
creations in Christ Jesus, qualified to do the work and will of our Father in heaven.

What we were destined to become—which speaks to our potential
and destiny. God has created in advance our destiny and potential expressed through our "Greater Yes!" We can live a life that echoes in
eternity.

The Path to True Greatness

The "Greater Yes!" becomes the means to demonstrate true greatness.
The descent to true greatness requires:

Unconditional love. Jesus could go down due to God's unconditional love for us. Christ demonstrated His love for us by making the
ultimate sacrifice on the cross. Should we do any less than demonstrate our love by loving the unlovely, the downcast, the addicted, and
the poor? Paul summed it up best,

> *If I speak with human eloquence and angelic ecstasy but don't love,
> I'm nothing but the creaking of a rusty gate. If I speak God's Word
> with power, revealing all his mysteries and making everything plain
> as day, and if I have faith that says to a mountain "Jump," and it
> jumps, but I don't love, I'm nothing. If I give everything I own to the
> poor and even go to the stake to be burned as a martyr, but I don't
> love, I've gotten nowhere. So, no matter what I say, what I believe,
> and what I do, I'm bankrupt without love.*

1 Corinthians 13:1–3 MSG

Unapologetic humility. It is more about attitude than altitude. It is about my attitude when going down. We often think it is about taking the low road—and it can be—but you can take the low road and still not be humble. You can give up everything and still not be humble. I have known people who seemed humble, and they were proud of it. It is more a state of mind than a place or position.

True humility is demonstrated by putting others first. *Don't push your way to the front; don't sweet-talk your way to the top. Put yourself aside, and help others get ahead. Don't be obsessed with getting your own advantage. Forget yourselves long enough to lend a helping hand* (Ph 2:3–4 MSG).

Uncompromising servanthood. The role of the servant is not only the best way to live, but the *only* way to live. When you begin to practice servanthood, you live the way of the cross. You become a living sacrifice, holy and acceptable in God's sight.

If you are going to be a servant: *Think of yourselves the way Christ Jesus thought of himself. He had equal status with God but didn't think so much of himself that he had to cling to the advantages of that status no matter what. Not at all. When the time came, he set aside the privileges of deity and took on the status of a slave* (Ph 2:5–7, MSG).

Servanthood is about position that is worked out after love and humility are worked in. It is how we live out our "Greater Yes!"

When we demonstrate unconditional love, unapologetic humility, and uncompromising servanthood, we will live a life that goes down instead of up. We will see the people who are serving us, the people in our workplace, the people we meet every day, in a new way. They're not great in the eyes of the world, but they are the most important people. They are the ones who need you to wash their feet and show them the full extent of God's love.

Someday you'll stand before God, and it will be God who says you're great. "Well done my good and faithful servant, you were faithful in what matters to me and gave up your lesser yeses for my 'Greater Yes!'" That's what I want. I want God to tell me I'm great. I don't care if the world tells me that.

If we are willing to lose it all, give it all up, we gain what really matters, that which is truly great. What is really great is what God says about me, what my wife says about me, and what my kids and grandkids and the people I serve in the ministry say about me. That's what really matters.

When Cathy and I started to think and talk about our "Greater Yes!", God made it clear that it was to be about loving and serving people because they matter most. So we named our ministry People Matter Ministries. If you do not believe people matter most, you will never find true greatness. We are the Chief Servant Leaders (CSL) of People Matter Ministries. That is a position we should strive to hold more than CEO.

Are you willing to lose it all in order to gain it all? Are you willing to descend in order to ascend? Moving down is the only way to become great in God's eyes, and nothing else matters. It is not the best path to greatness; it is the only path to true greatness.

Imagine the possibilities!

MOVING TOWARD MY "GREATER YES!"

1. What is keeping me from going down?

2. What part of the path do I lack?

3. What is God asking me to do that will demand I go down?

4. Who am I not willing to serve if God asked me?

5. What have I learned that will help me move toward my "Greater Yes!"?

MY PRAYER OF COMMITMENT

Loving heavenly Father, thank You for sending Your Son Jesus Christ to show us true greatness. Help me to be a servant, to humble myself and descend so I can be used by You. I lay aside those things that the world tells me are greatness in order to take up humility. Amen.

～ CHAPTER 25 ～

Giving Away the Blessing

You have to give yourself away.

If you could give only one thing to the people you love, what would it be? What would represent you and leave a lasting impression in their minds?

There is one gift that keeps on giving—God's blessing. We can give our loved ones things that wear out and are used up, or we can give them something that will last their whole lives.

I have made it my mission to give away God's blessing. When I shake someone's hand, give a hug, send an e-mail, or just converse, I always say, "Bless you!" Why? Because I know that what I am willing to give away comes back to me a hundred times. Besides, I am incredibly blessed. I don't want God's blessings going rotten in my life or hands. They are given to me to give away.

Bestowing divine favor is the greatest gift one can give. You might be thinking, "Wait a minute. I thought only God could bless people." Well, take a look inside yourself. Do you see God? As believers, we are like God in the flesh. We carry his blessing to the people and the places we go to every day. It's all semantics, anyway. I say "Bless you," you can say "God Bless You" if you'd rather, because any authority an individual has to bless another person comes from God. Either way, we can be an instrument of blessing no matter where we live or play.

It's important to remember, however, that you can't teach what you don't know, you can't lead where you've never gone, and you only reproduce what you are. If you don't personally appropriate God's blessing in your life, you have nothing to give to your family, your church, your children, your friends, or the lost world.

In Exodus 16, we find the Israelites wandering around in the wilderness. It only took a day to get the children of Israel out of Egypt, but it took forty years to get Egypt out of the children of Israel. They had started murmuring as soon as they got into the desert. They kept looking back to the past. So God provided manna and quail for them to eat, but they were only allowed to take enough for that day, or it would rot and be full of maggots the next morning.

We can be set free from our sins in a day, but God keeps trying to deal with the flesh in us. Most of us are still living our new life by old principles, and we're hoarding God's blessings like the Israelites hoarded the manna. The blessings God gives us were never meant for us to keep—they were meant for us to share. By faith we give, and then God gives the increase.

The Israelites marched around the wilderness for forty years, yet their shoes and their clothes never wore out, because God supplied their needs. In Philippians 4:19, Paul wrote: *My God will meet all your needs according to his glorious riches in Christ Jesus.* Everything we have comes from God—we just need to give God the credit for it.

We can live this new life by new principles, with new values, and new importance. In Ephesians 1:3, Paul wrote to the church: *Praise be to the God and Father of our Lord Jesus Christ, who has blessed us in the heavenly realms with every spiritual blessing in Christ"* God has given us every spiritual blessing without exception. In fact, because God sees us as He sees Jesus Christ, every spiritual blessing He gave to Christ, He gives to us. So we actually become the instruments of God's blessing on earth, just like Christ was.

Receiving God's Blessings

In my study of scripture, I looked at every passage that had the word "blessing" in it—nearly 220 of them—and I began to list how we appropriate God's blessing in our life. These are important to understand when deploying our "Greater Yes!

Here are just a few:

- Walk blamelessly and uprightly (Ps 1:1; 32:12; Pr 20:7; Is 56:2; Ma 5:8)
- Trust God (Ps 2:12; 34:8; 40:4; 84:12; Pr 16:20; 28:14; Je 17:7; Jo 20:29)
- Walk in forgiveness (Ps 32:1; Ro 4:7; Re 22:14)
- Be generous (Ps 37:26; Pr 22:9)
- Help the weak and needy (Ps 41:1; Pr 14:21; Ma 5:3; Lk 6:20; 14:14–15)

- Worship God (Ps 65:4; 89:15)
- Find your strength and confidence in God (Ps 84:4–5; 146:5)
- Fear the Lord (Ps 112:1; 128:1, 4)
- Keep God's commandments (Ps 119:2; Pr 29:18)
- Maintain justice (Ps 94:12)
- Listen to God (Pr 8:34)
- Be faithful (Pr 28:20)
- Hunger and thirst for righteousness (Ma 5:6; Lk 6:20)
- Be a peacemaker (Ma 5:9)
- Put your hope in God (Tit 2:13)
- Persevere under trials and suffering (Jam 1:12; 5:11; 1 Pe 3:14)
- See what God sees, feel what God feels, do what God does (Jo 13:1–17; Mk 6:33–44; Jo 6:1–14; Ph 2:1–11)

When we do these things, we are blessed! God then makes us instruments of His blessings. We can speak blessing and potential on behalf of God in the lives of people.

Your Blessing + Your Giving Away = Your "Greater Yes!"

Giving God's Blessings

Now that we know we have the blessing, to whom do we give it? Jesus told us to *"Love the Lord your God with all your heart and with all your soul and with all your mind. Love your neighbor as yourself"* (Ma 22:37, 39).

First, we are to **bless God**. David declared: *Bless the LORD, O my soul!* (Ps 104:1 NASB). How do we bless God? By appropriating His blessings in our life and by worshiping and giving a sacrifice of praise.

Second, we are to **bless our neighbors**. That includes our spouse, our family, the people who live next door, across the street, in our town, and around the world. Remember the story of the Good Samaritan? Even our enemies can be included in this category.

Third, we are to **bless ourselves**. Do you know God wants to bless you? Jabez prayed: *Oh, that you would bless me and enlarge my territory! Let your hand be with me* (1 Ch 4:10).

The other question is what makes up the kind of blessing we need to give? Our time, our talent, our treasure, and our meaningful, appropriate touch. What do you have that you can bless somebody else with?

One of the neighborhood kids came home from college for

Thanksgiving, and he came over and asked me, "Do you have any yard work I could do for you?"

I said, "Yeah, I've got a lot of leaves because my leaf guy didn't show up."

He studied me for a minute and said, "Twenty dollars."

I replied, "Tell you what. You do all the leaves and trust me, I will take care of you."

"What? What does that mean?" he asked

"Just trust me. Now we could settle for $20 right now or you can just trust me."

So he raked up all the leaves, and when he was done, I handed him $50. He got a big smile on his face. I was able to bless him with a little of my treasure.

We have a great van that is our second car, and we sometimes loan it out to people. That van has seen the United States, but not with me in it. It has been all over the country as various people have called me up and said, "Hey, I hear you loan out your van. Our van broke down and we're supposed to go on vacation tomorrow." So we let them borrow it, and then they return it, and we loan it out to the next person.

God gives you time, talent, treasure, and touch—and we each have our own unique ways in those areas with which we can bless people. What are some of yours? Are you blessing people with them? Or are you holding on to that blessing? If you hold on to it, the blessing will rot in your hands because it was never meant for you to hang on to.

Maybe you're retired, and you have the blessing of time. Are you investing it? Do you have a special ability? God says, "Invest it." If we live the new life by new principles, and we've appropriated God's blessing in our own life, we become the instruments of God's blessing on this earth.

My wife and I have been married for more than thirty-five years, and she has supported me in ministry, put me through seminary, and raised our kids. Now, it's my turn to support her. She has a heart for single moms. Almost half of the children in America will be in a single-parent home at some point, mostly led by the mothers, yet very few single moms even go to church. So my wife and I have decided to give the blessing of our resources to minister to single moms.

Think about your blessings. Which ones are you hanging onto? I guarantee that if you start blessing those around you, you will reap the benefits. It opens up the floodgates of heaven so God can give you more blessings. God can bless us with things on earth, but eternal blessings are the intangibles. Things rust, break, wear out and need to be replaced; the intangibles echo in eternity.

My parents have never had a lot of financial resources here on earth, but they have been blessed in countless other ways, including having all five of their children walking with God and in ministry. My dad would say, "I can't take it with me, but I can send it ahead." The real blessings will be experienced in heaven. We give ourselves away by faith, out of obedience to God, and we know we'll be blessed in return. What we don't know is exactly how. That's where trust, dependency, and contentment come in.

Principles for Giving Away Your Blessing

When you think about the need for giving away your blessing, remember it's not about you, and it's not about now. We need to live in such a way that it demands an explanation and echoes in eternity. Fill in the blanks in these principles with whatever your blessing is.

The more important your   (Example: Money)   is to you, the more you will want to hang on to it. What is it that you're hanging onto? God is saying, "Let go." Talking is an important part of my ministry, and the more important the speaking opportunity, the more I want to control it instead of allowing the Holy Spirit to dictate what I say. I have to repent and realize my talk is a blessing I need to give away.

Observe your   (Example: Talents)   often so you know when it is getting rotten in your own hands. Is it your time, talent, treasure, or touch? Look at it often so you know when you need to let it go to keep it from rotting. If we ignore what we have and go on with life, we won't even realize it's rotting in our hands.

What keeps you from giving your   (Example: Touch)   away is often fear. Can you trust God to provide for your need? He gives us every spiritual blessing, so we must simply remember it's not really ours in the first place. I don't fear failure; I fear succeeding at the things that don't matter. Many of us are hanging onto things because they measure success for us, yet they're the things that don't matter.

Many of us keep investing our   (Example: Time)   in the same old ways but keep expecting different results. We ask God, "Why aren't you blessing me?" He says, "Well, you keep living the new life by old principles. How's that working for you?" We need to do things differently so we can reap a different result.

The quicker you are willing to let go of your __(Example: Career)__, the sooner you can enjoy your new blessing. As soon as we start giving away our blessings, God will have something fresh for us. We can be continually receiving and giving new blessings!

Savor the adventure and enjoy the taste your new blessings bring. The adventure happens when we let go and trust God.

The potential of your "Greater Yes!" will find its greatest fulfillment when you give it away. The greatest potential is not in hanging on; it's in letting go. I challenge you to start blessing people. You will never be disappointed.

How do we give away the blessing? It starts with seeing what God sees, feeling what He feels, and then doing what He does. Just like Jesus, we have to become nothing (Ph 2:5) to truly serve.

Christ made Himself nothing, and He did an amazing thing for us. If we would make ourselves nothing, we can become an instrument of God's blessing wherever we live, work, or play. Your fingerprint of potential is found in the impressions of blessing you leave behind. Give yourself away.

Imagine the possibilities!

MOVING TOWARD MY "GREATER YES!"

1. What blessings has God given to me that He wants me to give away?

2. What keeps me from giving away my blessings?

3. Whom do I know who needs a blessing?

4. What am I trying to succeed at that does not matter?

5. What have I learned that will help me move toward my "Greater Yes!"?

MY PRAYER OF COMMITMENT

Heavenly Father, thank You for all the blessings in my life. Help me let go of my time, talent, treasure, and touch in order to bless the lives of those around me. I want to experience fresh blessings from You. Show me opportunities to be blessed by being a blessing. Amen.

≈ CHAPTER 26 ≈

Making an Impact

You have to mark where God is moving.

I carry some coffee stir sticks around in my backpack because I want to remember that I need to be a stir stick. I want to get into the lives of people and stir them up and help them reach their potential and become all God wants them to be.

Even though I'm over fifty, I believe the best years of my life are ahead of me. I'm not going to stand still and watch life go by.

What gets you up in the morning? What stirs your coffee? Do you have the initiative to attempt great things for God? You can create fire by striking a match, and, in the right environment, you could burn off the dried leaves and undergrowth from a whole forest, removing the main tinder that lets forest fires get out of hand and become terribly destructive. Your small light could ignite a salutary flame that spreads across the country. But Satan does not want us to ignite the country—he wants to keep our little lights stuck in a container.

God is calling us to initiate something, to become a stir stick. We don't want to reach the ends of our lives and say, "What did I really do for the Kingdom? What did I do for my family? What did I do for my work? What did I do that echoed in eternity?"

I challenge you to attempt something so great that if God is not in it, it is doomed for failure. Don't fear failure; only fear succeeding at things that don't matter. Whether you're a plumber or a lawyer or an Indian chief, God is more concerned about what He's doing in you than what He's doing with you and through you. He knows if He can stir a fire within you, He can change whatever you do. He can use you in anything you do.

Are you ready to ignite your "Greater Yes!"? Do you have a vision? The real tragedy for believers is not the sins we commit, it's the lives we fail to live.

I want you to consider three questions:

1. How would your life change if you really got involved, if you really took initiative, if you risked failure in order to do something meaningful?
2. Can you look back and remember moments that would have changed your life forever if you had made a different choice?
3. Do you live life or do you simply watch it?

Your Faith + Your "Greater Yes!" = Eternal Impact

Can't Just Sit There

In 1 Samuel 14, we find Saul and Jonathan in a lot of trouble. They are in the midst of a battle against the Philistines, yet Saul and his men are sitting under a pomegranate tree, sleeping. God is on their side, so they have the advantage, but they are just hanging out.

That's where Satan loves to keep us—in the barracks, in a secure place, away from the battle. We have the resources and the power, but we need to get out into battle!

In the last chapter, we looked at how our blessing can rot if we hold onto it. That's what was happening to Saul. He had everything he needed to win the battle, but he was holding onto it. He was sleeping under the pomegranate tree.

However, Jonathan decided to take action. He woke up his armor-bearer and said, "Let's go get these guys!" Jonathan wasn't going to just sit there.

Erwin McManus wrote in *Seizing Your Divine Moment*,

> *Those who hold the authority and the resources of the kingdom are all too often more motivated to make sure they do not lose them rather than to make sure they are used properly...The greatest danger that success brings, aside from arrogance, is the fear of losing what has been gained...The more you move with God-given urgency, the more God seems to bless your life. The more God blesses your life, the more you have to lose. The more you have to lose, the more you have to risk. The more you have to risk, the higher the price of following God. In some twisted way, God's blessings to us can become our greatest hindrances to seizing our divine moments.*[1]

What is God dreaming in you? What keeps you up at night? What gets you up in the morning? How are you going to build the kingdom of God? What is keeping you from sleep sometimes, driving you to your knees? What is stirring you up?

To Initiate or Not to Initiate

Here are a few of the main things that keep us from making an impact:

We get stuck in a rut. Like Saul, we're sitting under a tree, protecting the life we have, instead of attempting what God really wants us to do. We relinquish our opportunity to seize our divine destiny. What is your pomegranate tree? Where do you find security? What rut are you stuck in?

We get stuck in the past (1 Sa 24). I was teaching my first granddaughter to swing on the monkey bars and she got caught in the middle. I told her to let go, but she said, "No, Papa. I'm afraid."

"Just try it. Trust me. I won't let you fall," I told her. So she let go, and fell right into my arms. Now she can swing all the way across without any help. She has forgotten the past and pushed ahead. In many ways, we get stuck in the past—our past accomplishments, our past failures, our past sins. All we need to do is trust God, let go, and push ahead with confidence.

We get stuck in neutral (1 Sa 5). When your car is in neutral, you can rev the engine all you want, but it still won't go anywhere. You'll be making a lot of noise, and life will just be passing you by. Is your life making a lot of noise, but going nowhere? A lot of us are living in neutral and going nowhere because we don't have a vision.

We get stuck on the sidelines. Church and ministries are much like a football game: there are 70,000 people in the stands who need the exercise and twenty-two people on the field who need rest. So many Christians are observing from the pews, sitting on the sidelines criticizing the pastor instead of getting in the game. We are called to stand out!

We get stuck in indifference. We become passive instead of passionate. God hates the lukewarm. What are you passionate about? Are you ready to respond to your calling?

We get stuck in fear. Jonathan was willing to take a risk. He was willing to make himself visible. The only way we're ever going to ignite is if we get out from under the pomegranate tree and face the enemy.

Characteristics of Those Who Make an Impact

Four words separate those who watch life go by from those who make an impact. Jonathan said: *Come, let us go* (1 Sa 14:6 NKJV). Are you willing to say those four words? God is saying, "Come, just try. Initiate. Take the chance. Take the risk. Step out. I will take care of you. I will give you the battle."

Those who initiate have these characteristics:

They act. When we act, life invades our space, it intrudes on our comfort, it interrupts our apathy, and it forces our response. When Jonathan was willing to climb through that valley and face the enemy, his comfort was gone. Taking the initiative to act, instead of merely reacting, can make the difference.

They risk. Jonathan took a big risk in stepping out from the safety of the rest of the army. Taking initiative will almost always require risk, but it will always be worth it.

They display courage and character. Initiators are not weak—they have to be ready to make tough decisions.

They make a difference. Initiators do not allow their circumstances to limit the impact of their life. I remember Joni Eareckson Tada, whose dive into a lake broke her neck and made her a quadriplegic. Despite her circumstances (and probably because of them), her life has been an incredible blessing over the years. She has written books and started a successful ministry because she did not allow her injury to dictate her impact.

If you allow the past to dictate the present, you'll never go to the future. That's why we have to forgive and forget. You may be in a great business or job but feel like a failure. You can still make a difference. Sometimes God pulls you up by the roots, and moves you halfway across the country to minister to the Indians. Probably more often God says, "I want you to make an impact where you are."

They obey God when God speaks. We will always make an impact when we obey God. He will never ask us to just sit and watch our lives go by. He wants us to get up and ignite a fire that will spread and impact people all around us.

They seize their divine moments. Initiators do not miss divine opportunities to make an impact. They see when God is working and they are at the forefront of what He is getting ready to do.

They inspire others to greatness. If you're going to be a stir stick, you need to stir others to greatness. Those who make an impact are leaders who bring others alongside them and inspire them to find their "Greater Yes!" as well.

Don't choose to do nothing. Find out what God is doing and birthing in you. Ask yourself, "If I had unlimited resources and complete freedom to fail, what would I attempt for God?" Ask God to begin to give you a "Greater Yes!" and then surround yourself with people who will encourage you to develop that dream.

I was talking with someone about a business he wanted to expand, which is great! But I said, "Can you use that business for the kingdom? How would that look?" Maybe what you are already doing can become your tool to make an impact.

While everyone else slept, Jonathan woke up and took action. He decided to make a difference in his world. You and I can make a difference, too. Maybe it seems crazy to think that we could somehow change the course of human history. But if it's normal to wake up in the morning and just try to make it through the day, then I vote for abnormality.

I want to change my world, and I believe God can use you to change your world, but you've got to ignite. Catch on fire and people will come to watch you burn. You need to initiate a "Greater Yes!" that can echo and make an impact for now and into eternity. God can change the world through you.

Imagine the possibilities!

MOVING TOWARD MY "GREATER YES!"

1. What kind of impact would I like to make for eternity?

2. What is keeping me from making a greater impact?

3. Am I seeing the results of making an eternal impact?

4. What are some of the eternal impacts I am making right now?

5. What have I learned that will help me move toward my "Greater Yes!"?

My Prayer of Commitment

Thank you, Father, for giving me a dream, a "Greater Yes!" Help me to see how I can use it to make an impact in my world. I don't want to stand and watch my life drift by; I want to take a risk and seize my divine moment. Put Your fire in me so I can ignite others and start a fire in the church that won't go out. Amen.

CHAPTER 27

Never Give Up!

You have to never give up.

Winston Churchill was invited to give a speech at his old grade school, Harrow School, for their commencement. In it he said, "Never give in, never give in, never, never, never, never—in nothing, great or small, large or petty, never give in except to convictions of honor and good sense. Never yield to fear, never yield to apparently overwhelming might of the enemy."[1] What great wisdom from a man who never, never, never, never gave up.

Paul once wrote to the church at Thessalonica:

You need to know, friends, that thanking God over and over for you is not only a pleasure; it's a must. We have to do it. Your faith is growing phenomenally; your love for each other is developing wonderfully. Why, it's only right that we give thanks. We're so proud of you; you're so steady and determined in your faith despite all the hard times that have come down on you. We tell everyone we meet in the churches all about you.

2 Thessalonians 1:3–4 MSG

The key to making your "Greater Yes!" more than just a dream is perseverance. You must persist in a purpose; continue striving in spite of opposition or difficulties.

The opposite of perseverance is giving up. By giving up I don't mean simply quitting. I know people who are still doing their jobs, but they have given up trying to find satisfaction in them. Some people haven't quit their marriages yet, but they have given up on them. They've settled for dissatisfaction instead of persevering through God's power, to all He has promised for them.

It's tempting to give up on situations because we get tired and worn

184

out. Have you ever felt surrounded by enemies, or in a tough situation the solution for which seems out of reach? Do you just want to stay in bed sometimes because there is no reason to get up?

The apostle Paul had more than enough reasons to give up. He was beaten, stoned, imprisoned, mocked, and ridiculed, and still he persevered. So that the church in Corinth would understand the sort of travails he had faced and survived, he wrote to them:

> *Five times I received from the Jews the forty lashes minus one. Three times I was beaten with rods, once I was stoned, three times I was shipwrecked, I spent a night and a day in the open sea, I have been constantly on the move. I have been in danger from rivers, in danger from bandits, in danger from my own countrymen, in danger from Gentiles; in danger in the city, in danger in the country, in danger at sea; and in danger from false brothers. I have labored and toiled and have often gone without sleep; I have known hunger and thirst and have often gone without food; I have been cold and naked. Besides everything else, I face daily the pressure of my concern for all the churches.*
>
> 2 Corinthians 11:24–28

Yet with all these things, Paul was still able to say, *For Christ's sake, I delight in weaknesses, in insults, in hardships, in persecutions, in difficulties. For when I am weak, then I am strong* (2 Co 12:10).

Difficult things will come your way eventually, if they haven't already. However, you can plan ahead to persevere through any situation.

Three times Paul went to God and asked for deliverance from the thorn in his flesh (2 Co 12:7–9). Theologians have speculated about what the thorn might have been and whether it was physical or not. The important thing to note is that God told Paul, "My grace is sufficient for you." Paul realized he gained strength in his weakness, because it's when we go down that God can use us.

In the second book of Kings we find a woman who really had her back against a wall. Her husband, the provider of the family, had died, and her boys were being taken into slavery to satisfy her husband's debts. So she went and *cried out to Elisha*, God's prophet (2 Ki 4:1).

Elisha replied to her, "How can I help you? Tell me, what do you have in your house?" (v. 2). Elisha sent the widow to get what was inside her house. God is always going to point to what's inside of us.

"Your servant has nothing there at all," she said, "except a little oil."
Elisha said, "Go around and ask all your neighbors for empty jars.
Don't ask for just a few. Then go inside and shut the door behind
you and your sons. Pour oil into all the jars, and as each is filled,
put it to one side." She left him and afterward shut the door behind
her and her sons. They brought the jars to her and she kept pouring.
When all the jars were full, she said to her son, "Bring me another
one." But he replied, "There is not a jar left." Then the oil stopped
flowing. She went and told the man of God, and he said, "Go, sell
the oil and pay your debts. You and your sons can live on what is
left."

2 Kings 4:2–7

What to Do When You're Up Against a Wall

This story is full of great principles that can apply to us when we find
ourselves in a dismal situation.

Cry out to the source. The widow went to the man of God, the
prophet Elisha. When you go to the right source—the authority of
God, the presence of God, the Word of God—you will find the way
out of your tough situation.

Remember, God's voice is the still, small one. The world yells at us
through commercials, spam e-mails, and junk mail, telling us the solution is to just get more money, new stuff, or a different relationship.
Well, ask the movie stars and sports heroes who have all kinds of
money, possessions, and relationships, and I bet many of them would
say they are still up against walls in their personal lives.

Before you go to God, you'll be offered all kinds of e-mails from Satan telling you what you ought to do to deal with your situation.
Don't listen to them. Go straight to God and his Word for the solution. God allows us to get into those hard places because he has a work
to do in us. We short-circuit God's work in us when we become our
own deliverer.

Go to the right place. The solution to the widow's dilemma was actually right where she was. Look into your spiritual house—what do
you have? A little bit of hope, a little faith, can go a long way when
you let God start working through it.

What counsel does the world offer us? If you can't make it in your
marriage, leave your spouse. You can get another marriage. If you can't
make it in your job, leave that job. If that church is too convicting, go

to one that isn't. When your back is against the wall, Satan doesn't want you dealing with the real issues that put you there or finding your true deliverance.

Practice right obedience. Don't try to understand and analyze your situation before you take action, or you'll never get started. Just be faithful to God's Word and don't let doubt make you stumble and fall. Instead of dwelling on what may have caused your present circumstances, you need to press forward, obeying God's Word.

The widow did exactly what Elisha told her. Can you imagine how she must have looked going to all the neighbors and saying, "Do you have any empty jars? I don't know what I'm doing with them, but Elisha told me to collect them."

Obeying God isn't easy, especially when His direction is illogical from the world's perspective. Our world would've told the widow that collecting jars doesn't make sense but indulging herself a little does. Maybe some wine would help her relax. Working extra hours will keep her mind off her loss. Letting her sons go would free her to pursue her own plans. But we know self-indulgence has never solved a problem. The widow's simple obedience instead of self-indulgence had a big payoff for her.

I was counseling a man who had been married for twenty-six years and wanted to leave his wife. When I asked him why, he gave me a whole list of excuses, but it just came down to, "She doesn't make me feel good anymore." That's the bottom line, isn't it? We all think the grass is greener on the other side. I'll let you in on a little secret: the grass on the other side isn't greener, it's just Astroturf. We need to stay on our side of the fence, where God has placed us, and persevere in obedience to Him, even if it doesn't make sense from the world's perspective.

Listen to the right people. Beware of power doubters and praise poopers. Do you have any of those around you? Who is giving you advice in your life? Who is robbing you of trusting in God's power or giving Him praise? Who is around you when your back is against the wall? How you get through that situation will be partly determined by who's around you.

Make sure you have enough jars. The widow didn't collect the number of jars she thought was enough. She kept going and going until she and all her neighbors had not a single jar left. As long as the jars kept coming, so did the oil. How much do we trust God? Do we ask for His help only in little things we think aren't too hard for Him? Or do we fling open every area of pain, need and weakness with the ex-

pectation that He will answer to overflowing? I'd rather give everything to Him than bits and pieces. He wants to give us all of His oil,
but we have to give Him every jar in our lives.

Paul encouraged us: *We have this treasure in jars of clay to show that
this all-surpassing power is from God and not from us. We are hard pressed
on every side, but not crushed; perplexed, but not in despair; persecuted,
but not abandoned; struck down, but not destroyed* (2 Co 4:7–9).

In light of that, we could say having our back against the wall is the
normal Christian life. But listen to how Paul described the hope we
have in spite of it:

> *Therefore we do not lose heart. Though outwardly we are wasting
> away, yet inwardly we are being renewed day by day. For our light
> and momentary troubles are achieving for us an eternal glory that
> far outweighs them all. So we fix our eyes not on what is seen, but
> on what is unseen. For what is seen is temporary, but what is un-
> seen is eternal.*
>
> 2 Corinthians 4:16–18

God promises that our "empty jar" situations are temporary and
will work out for our eternal good.

Remember you can't do it alone. Get with a group of fellow believers. I saw a television show one time that described how the army puts
together some special forces. They train one guy to know about medicine, one to know about communication, one to know all about
weapons, and one to know about engineering. Then they send them
out in those groups of four, and if they get injured, they've got a med-
ical guy; if they need to blow something up, they've got an engineering guy, etc. We all need each others' specialties.

Caleb was one of ten spies who went into the Promised Land. He
and Joshua said, *We should go up and take possession of the land for we
can certainly do it* (Nu 13:30). But the children of Israel, lacking faith,
refused to enter the Promised Land, and after forty years, everyone died
in the wilderness except Caleb and Joshua. Because they kept their faith
and never gave up, they entered into the land of promise.

Caleb later told Joshua:

> *"I, however, followed the LORD my God wholeheartedly. Now then,
> just as the Lord promised, he has kept me alive for forty-five years
> since the time he said this to Moses, while Israel moved about in the
> desert. So here I am today, eighty-five years old! I am still as strong*

*today as the day Moses sent me out; I am just as vigorous to go out
to battle now as I was then."*

Joshua 14:8b,10–11

I invite you to never give up, never, never, never, never in anything
great or small. Never yield to fear; never yield to the apparently overwhelming might of the enemy. Look to Jesus, the author and finisher
of your "Greater Yes!"

Imagine the possibilities!

Your Perseverance + Your Potential = Your "Greater Yes!"

MOVING TOWARD MY "GREATER YES!"

1. What has forced my back against a wall?

2. What am I ready to give in to or give up on?

3. What have I learned from God's faithfulness that can help me now?

4. What character is God trying to develop in my life through my need for perseverance?

5. What have I learned that will help me move toward my "Greater Yes!"?

MY PRAYER OF COMMITMENT

*God, thank You for being there when my back is up against a wall. I know
You are using my hardships to help me grow and learn to trust You more.
Help me never give up as You stretch me and develop the character of
Christ in my life. Amen.*

CHAPTER 28

Finishing Well!

*You have to realize it is about how you end the race,
not how you start it.*

During a long flight, I was thinking about what it would be like to be in heaven when I felt my eyes begin to grow heavy. I settled into my seat and started to drift off. In my imagination, I saw myself standing before God in His throne room.

Sitting at his right hand was Jesus Christ. When I saw the Savior for the first time, I began to weep with joy. I wanted so much to embrace Him and express my love to Him. I had lived my whole life for this day. God was smiling.

Jesus rose and reached out His hands to mine, and as we embraced I could feel the scars. He whispered, "Welcome home," wiping away my tears while I looked around to see millions of saints who had come before—they were all rejoicing for me!

Then two figures came from the shadows of the throne, and with delight I recognized them as my dad and mom. They looked the same, but different, with crowns of indescribable glory and beauty upon their heads. As we embraced, I noticed there were no more tears, only joy and deep satisfaction.

Then God stood, the praise quieted, and He motioned for me to come forward. He had a father's smile and loving eyes that seemed to pierce my very soul. As I moved toward Him, I could feel my heart and knees beginning to go low before Him while my head bowed in reverence and awe. I had never felt taller than when I was on my knees before the Almighty.

When God finally spoke, it was as if all of heaven stood in silence. He spoke only to me. "Dan, you are my son, whom I love, and in whom I am well pleased. You have finished well! You have been a faithful servant! Since you have been faithful with a few things, I will put you in charge of many things. Come and share our happiness!"

Raising my head, I watched as God placed a magnificent crown upon my head while the multitude of saints from every tribe and tongue began to take up their rejoicing again. When I rose, I was standing with Peter, James, John, and others. They congratulated me and acted as if they knew me, as if they had been watching me.

Then Peter said, "Look, Dan," and I saw many others coming toward the throne. To my amazement and joy, I recognized them—my son, Doug, his wife, Ginny, my daughter, Shannon, her husband Rusty, my grandchildren, men from my discipleship groups over the years, my brothers and sister, my small group, Ed, Reed, and Bob, single moms, and so many others. They kept hugging me and thanking me. It was like a family reunion.

Then everyone stopped and the crowd parted to reveal the most wonderful sight I had ever seen. Coming toward me, looking more beautiful than the first day I laid eyes on her, was my wife, Cathy. I ran to her, and we embraced, and I whispered, "I love you so much. Welcome home." She looked up at me with a smile and a gleam in her blue eyes, and said, "Nice crown. It's my turn."

Joining hands, we walked toward the throne of God while the crowd gathered behind. Again, I could see God smiling and Jesus weeping, and I thought, "This is going to be a terrific eternity!"

My silent reverie was probably only a glimmer of what heaven will be like. God is calling us to finish well. We can't change how we started—we did not choose our parents, nationality, ethnic group, gender, or status in life—but we can define and determine our finish. We can choose our final destiny.

Paul knew what it meant to devote your life to finishing well. He wrote:

You've all been to the stadium and seen the athletes race. Everyone runs; one wins. Run to win. All good athletes train hard. They do it for a gold medal that tarnishes and fades. You're after one that's gold eternally. I don't know about you, but I'm running hard for the finish line. I'm giving it everything I've got. No sloppy living for me! I'm staying alert and in top condition. I'm not going to get caught napping, telling everyone else all about it and then missing out myself.

1 Corinthians 9:24–27 MSG

What is it going to take to finish well? After studying all the major players in the story of redemption found in the Bible, including Christ, I have concluded there are three consistent qualities we need to have in our lives in order to both run and finish well.

Conviction

While in seminary, I was working for an equipment dealer. One day my boss came to me and said, "Hey, Dan, just don't tell the customers everything about the used equipment. Tell them only enough so they will still buy the equipment."

I got up out of my chair calmly, put my hands in my pocket, looked at him, and said, "I'm not going to lie for you or anyone else."

All of a sudden, my conviction became more important than my job. Convictions are more important than the demands people or circumstances put on you. There are not enough of us standing up saying, "I'm going to stick to my convictions even if it costs me my career, my friends, my position, or anything else."

Conviction can be defined as fixed or unshakeable belief. What is always in conflict with conviction? Compromise! In Genesis 12, Abraham left his God-given convictions in Canaan and took a detour down into Egypt. There he compromised and almost gave his wife to Pharaoh.

Have you ever battled compromise in your life? There are situations when it is prudent to compromise, but not when we have to compromise God's truth, our thought life, our morality, or our integrity.

Have you ever cheated? Maybe sneaked a peak at some answers on a test in school? Or just kind of stretched it a little bit on your tax returns? I have, and the Holy Spirit has convicted me. Have you ever robbed God? When that happens, the Holy Spirit convicts us. Once it becomes a conviction we live by, it doesn't have to convict us any longer. What are you convicted about? Or do you compromise so much that you're barely convicted about anything?

How do you determine what is really conviction? It is revealed by how you invest your time and energy, your talent and influence, your priorities and possessions—whether for your own purposes or God's. We are supposed to live out our convictions. Where are our priorities? How do we spend our time and money? That will demonstrate where our true convictions lie.

Courage

Courage can be defined as a quality of spirit that enables us to face danger or pain without showing fear. We can have courage even when the circumstances call for anxiety and fear.

Joshua knew all about reasons to fear when he inherited Moses' leadership position over the people of Israel. But God commanded Joshua,

> *Be strong and courageous, because you will lead these people to inherit the land I swore to their forefathers to give them. Be strong and very courageous...Have I not commanded you? Be strong and courageous. Do not be terrified; do not be discouraged, for the LORD your God will be with you wherever you go.*

Joshua 1:6–7, 9

It's not "maybe you'll have success" or "if you do all the tricks right," or "if you send out all the right marketing, you'll have success." The promise from God is, "If you follow my Book, I will be with you—just like I was with Moses, Joshua, Paul, and Peter, and all the disciples and courageous men and women who have gone before."

What is the opposite of courage? Many people would say cowardice. But fear is not the issue. God knows we will all have fear, but courage is rising out of a fearful situation. The opposite of one who is courageous is one who simply does nothing. When presented with the question "Do you flee or do you fight?", most of us do neither. In Revelation 3, God said He would rather have you cold toward Him (cowardly) or hot for Him (courageous) than neutral and do nothing.

Courage always relates to action. There is always an enemy involved. It's dangerous to get up each morning and not even contemplate the fact that there is an enemy and a fight ahead of us. We look at the enemy and think, "He won't bother me if I don't bother him," and so we don't make a difference.

As soldiers of Christ, we don't want to be AWOL (absent without leave) or MIA (missing in action). God does not intend for us to be overwhelmed in the battle, nor to cower, but to define courage in the midst of battle.

Commitment

Commitment can be defined as binding to a course of action. Paul understood commitment and was concerned about how he finished his race. He wrote:

But there is another urgency before me now. I feel compelled to go to Jerusalem. I'm completely in the dark about what will happen when I get there. I do know that it won't be any picnic, for the Holy Spirit has let me know repeatedly and clearly that there are hard times and imprisonment ahead. But that matters little. What matters most to me is to finish what God started; the job the Master Jesus gave me of letting everyone I meet know all about this incredibly extravagant generosity of God.

Acts 20:22–24 MSG

Our society treats the idea of commitment so lightly. You commit as long as you feel right about it and the commitment doesn't come at a personal cost. If it's free and feels good, then, by all means, commit! Otherwise, move on.

In God's perspective, making a commitment means pledging to do something—it's really giving your life, your integrity, and your character as surety on a promise.

God is more concerned about His children being obedient than happy. For instance, wedding vows are a commitment to love the other person for better or for worse, in sickness and in health, not "until I fall out of love" or "as long as I'm happy."

If you are going to reach your God-given potential and destiny, you have to commit. Commitment is not conditional. "I'll commit as long as they're paying me right." "I'll commit as long as they're treating me right." "I'll commit as long as I'm feeling right." I've heard the excuse, "I'm not a morning person." Well, I'm not a morning, afternoon, or evening person—I just do whatever it takes to get the job done. If I have to get up, I get up.

Most people will never live their "Greater Yes!" because it will take commitment. You can say you are committed to the Lord, but if you don't spend your time, talent, treasure, and touch showing it, your life is saying otherwise. Only you can measure your commitment, but it is an important thing to do. God wants men and women to obey their convictions with truth and duty at the cost of fortune, fame, family, friends, or life itself.

Conviction + Courage + Commitment = Living and Finishing Well!

Is there enough evidence in your life that you could be charged with possession of conviction, courage, and commitment? Paul lays out what should be evident in your life and "Greater Yes!" if you are going to finish well: *We continually remember before God and Father your work produced by faith, your labor prompted by love, and your endurance inspired by hope in our Lord Jesus Christ* (1 Th 1:3).

Your work produced by faith. "I've done it in my own strength," Paul was saying. "Now I'm watching you guys imitate my faith." They knew faith in God was necessary to finish the race.

Your labor prompted by love. What motivates us to feel what we feel, say what we say, and do what we do? If all you do is not driven by love, it is nothing. *[Love] bears all things, believes all things, hopes all things, endures all things. Love never fails"* (1 Co 13:7–8 NASB)

Your endurance inspired by hope. Our hope is built on Jesus' blood and His righteousness. We are motivated to finish well by looking forward to His return.

Get Plugged In

Where is the power in life to have convictions, courage, and commitment? It comes from the Holy Spirit, who is ready to fill us up each day with His power. We just have to allow Him to empower us and stop trying to make so many of our decisions on our own. Let's get on our knees every day and ask Him to work powerfully through us. We'll never, ever be as tall as when we are on our knees.

I want to be a man who helps others to finish well. We cannot produce people of conviction, courage, and commitment if we're not living them out in our own lives. We need to understand three principles if we are going to finish well:

1. We can only teach what we know and experience.
2. We can only lead where we are willing to go.
3. We only reproduce who we are.

You can't reproduce children of morality if you're not a person of morality. You can't disciple others and train them to be men and women of God's Word if you're not a man or woman of the Word. I have to be honest—my kids struggle with that because I wasn't a man of the Word when they were in my home. I wasn't a man of prayer like I should have been. I was so busy working for Jesus that I wasn't allowing Him to work in my own life. But now I can stand and say, "I'm in the process."

The Bottom Line

Here is what it is going to take to finish well:

- We have to keep our focus on the prize, which is the Lord.

- We have to know and watch for the enemy (the devil, not other people).
- We must not believe Satan's lies.
- We have to remember that God will never leave us, or forsake us.
- We need to be the leaders we were meant to be.
- We must not get ahead of God.
- Remember, victory is assured.

When my dad decided to go to the reservation and minister to the Native Americans, I saw a man who had convictions, courage, and commitment. From the world's view, he didn't have the good looks, the prestige, the strength, or the talent, but he had God's call, and he made himself available.

He never gave up, even when he didn't have any money or resources. Through all the hardship, and all the things it took to stay there for thirty-eight years, never making more than $10,000 a year in his life, he built two churches and saw multitudes of Native Americans come to know Christ.

Now, at eighty-three years old, my dad says, "I'd never give it up. I would never exchange it for anything." That is a man who lived out his potential and destiny, his "Greater Yes!" Was he a perfect man? No. God is not calling perfect people; otherwise we'd all be in trouble. We are all "do-overs."

Paul told Timothy:

You take over. I'm about to die, my life an offering on God's altar. This is the only race worth running. I've run hard right to the finish, believed all the way. All that's left now is the shouting—God's applause! Depend on it, he's an honest judge. He'll do right not only by me, but everyone eager for his coming.

2 Timothy 4:6–8 MSG

God wants you to finish well! God wants to tell you, "You have been a faithful servant! Since you have been faithful with a few things, I will put you in charge of many things. Come and share our happiness!"

Imagine the possibilities!

Moving Toward My "Greater Yes!"

1. What is keeping you from finishing well?

2. What does finishing well mean to you?

3. What are the evidences in you life that you are finishing well?

4. What qualities (convictions, courage or commitment) do you need in your life in order to finish well?

5. What have I learned that will help me move toward my "Greater Yes!"?

My Prayer of Commitment

God, thank You for my "Greater Yes!" Help me to have the conviction, courage, and commitment to finish well so one day I can hear You say, "Well, done, good and faithful servant." That is my heart's desire. Amen.

SECTION 5

So What?
Where Do I Go from Here?

If you are ever going to move to what God has destined you to become, you have to have commitment. You can't wait. Don't remain stuck or in neutral.

I would encourage you get away on a personal retreat by yourself or with your mate or a small group of friends. There is a journey God will have you go through. He is more concerned about the process than the end result, and there are several areas to consider as you define, discover, develop, and deploy your "Greater Yes!"

You can live a life that realizes your God-given potential and destiny!

~ CHAPTER 29 ~

First Things First

Finding your "Greater Yes!" starts with a personal relationship with Jesus Christ!

Remember the rare eagle I observed in the cage at the zoo? He was created to soar over mountains with wings spread wide, yet there he was, sitting sadly on a branch—never to experience the power of his potential and destiny.

When God made all of the heavens and earth, He said it was "good." When He made mankind, He said it was "very good" (Ge 1:28–31). He said, "It was so good, so very good" (MSG). We became His "Greater Yes!" He loves us too much to keep us the way we are. If we are going to experience the power to reach our God-given potential and destiny, first things have to come first. We need a personal, intimate relationship with Jesus Christ.

I now want to give you a clear understanding of why God sent His Son to die on a cross for you and me.

We All Need a "Do Over"

> God did it for us. Out of sheer generosity he put us in right standing with Himself. A pure gift. He got us out of the mess we're in and restored us to where He always wanted us to be. And he did it by means of Jesus Christ.
>
> Romans 3:24 MSG

> It wasn't so long ago that you were mired in that old stagnant life of sin. You let the world, which doesn't know the first thing about living, tell you how to live. You filled your lungs with polluted unbelief, and then exhaled disobedience. We all did it, all of us doing

200

what we felt like doing, when we felt like doing it, all of us in the same boat. It's a wonder God didn't lose his temper and do away with the whole lot of us. Instead, immense in mercy and with an incredible love, he embraced us. He took our sin-dead lives and made us alive in Christ. He did all this on his own, with no help from us! Then he picked us up and set us down in highest heaven in company with Jesus, Our Messiah.

Ephesians 2:1–6 MSG

And we know that in all things God works for the good of those who love him, who have been called according to his purpose. For those God foreknew he also predestined to be conformed to the likeness of his Son, that he might be the firstborn among many brothers. And those he predestined, he also called; those he called, he also justified; those he justified, he also glorified.

Romans 8:28–30

God Loves Us Unconditionally

For God so loved the world that he gave his one and only Son, that whoever believes in him shall not perish but have eternal life (Jo 3:16).

But God demonstrates his own love for us in this: While we were still sinners, Christ died for us (Ro 5:8).

Christ is God's Provision for Eternal Life

For the wages of sin is death, but the gift of God is eternal life in Christ Jesus our Lord (Ro 6:23).

Salvation is found in no one else, for there is no other name under heaven given to men by which we must be saved (Ac 4:12).

For what I received I passed on to you as of first importance: that Christ died for our sins according to the Scriptures, that he was buried, that he was raised on the third day (1 Co 15:3–4).

God Has a Plan for Our Lives

If people can't see what God is doing, they stumble all over themselves; but when they attend to what he reveals, they are most blessed (Pr 29:18 MSG).

"For I know the plans I have for you," declares the LORD, "plans to prosper you and not to harm you, plans to give you hope and a future" (Je 29:11).

For we are God's workmanship, created in Christ Jesus to do good works, which God prepared in advance for us to do (Ep 2:10).

God Will Exchange

If anyone is in Christ, he is a new creation; the old has gone, the new has come! (2 Co 5:17). God wants to exchange the old for the new.

Old Creation	New Creation
Our rebellion	For His forgiveness
Our guilt	For His pardon
Our condemnation	For His mercy
Our sin	For His grace
Our failure	For His significance
Our bondage	For His freedom
Our broken	For His reconciliation
Our poverty	For His inheritance
Our unbelief	For His faith
Our discouragement	For His courage
Our turmoil	For His peace
Our thirst	For His living water
Our debt	For His redemption
Our despair	For His hope
Our conditional love	For His unconditional love

God Has Given Us a Promise

If we confess our sins, he is faithful and just and will forgive us our sins and purify us from all unrighteousness (1 Jo 1:9).

That if you confess with your mouth, "Jesus is Lord" and believe in your heart that God raised him from the dead, you will be saved (Ro 10:9).

"I tell you the truth, whoever hears my word and believes him who sent me has eternal life and will not be condemned; he has crossed over from death to life" (Jo 5:24).

Receive Jesus Christ by Faith through Prayer

Consider praying this prayer for the first time or in rededication:

Dear God, I confess that I have sinned. I know You sent Your Son to die on a cross for me. He took on my punishment. He rose from the dead on the third day and is now in heaven making intercession on my behalf. I receive You, Jesus Christ, as my Lord and Savior. Please come into my life. Thank You that I can know if I died tonight I would have eternal life in Christ Jesus. Amen.

MOVING TOWARD MY "GREATER YES!"

1. Do I have a personal relationship with Jesus Christ? If not, why?

2. Have I surrendered my life and destiny over to God? If not, why?

3. What is in my life that God needs to exchange?

4. Do I know God's plan for my life for now and for eternity?

5. What have I learned that will help me move toward my "Greater Yes!"?

MY PRAYER OF COMMITMENT

Father, I want to thank You for loving me unconditionally and giving me a do-over. Thank You for your gift of eternal life in Christ Jesus. Help me make Him both my Lord and Savior. Thank You that You have a wonderful plan for my life. May I find my "Greater Yes!" I know I can live a life that echoes in eternity. Amen.

➤ CHAPTER 30 ➤

Journey to Your "Greater Yes!"

The journey is as important as the destination!

Have you ever felt something so strongly that it kept you up at night? If you think about great men of God who have done great things, you'll see it all began with a vision God instilled in them.

As I sit down with men and coach them, a lot of times they want to talk about the now, and I want to talk to them about eternity. Your vision must be in light of eternity. Finding your "Greater Yes!" means seeking to define, discover, develop, and deploy your potential and destiny. God didn't save you just so you would not go to hell.

I was coaching a young man, and I asked him, "If you had unlimited resources and complete freedom to fail, what would you trust God to do with and through you for now and eternity?"

He said, "Well, I would go to Ecuador as a missionary."

So I asked, "Why don't you do that?" He began to list all the reasons why he couldn't. I said, "Well, I guess God's not in the picture. You don't think God can take care of any of your excuses?"

He looked at me and said, "What do you think I need to do to find my 'Greater Yes!'?" I shared with him some of what I've shared with you in this book, and two years later, he was in Ecuador as a missionary. He needed someone to believe—and help *him* believe—that he could reach his God-given potential.

What do you think God wants to do in and through you? I would be disappointed if you read this book and stayed the same. God loves you too much to keep you the way you are. I don't care if you're young or old—there is destiny written on your heart by God.

Paul knew what it took for the journey toward his "Greater Yes!" He wrote:

I'm not saying that I have this all together, that I have it made. But I am well on my way, reaching out for Christ, who has so wondrously reached out for me. Friends, don't get me wrong: By no means do I count myself an expert in all of this, but I've got my eye on the goal, where God is beckoning us onward—to Jesus. I'm off and running, and I'm not turning back. So let's keep focused on that goal, those of us who want everything God has for us. If any of you have something else in mind, something less than total commitment, God will clear your blurred vision—you'll see it yet! Now that we're on the right track, let's stay on it.

Philippians 3:12-16 MSG

Misconceptions

What keeps you from embracing and pursuing your God-given potential and destiny? What is keeping you from pressing on to the goal to which God has called you in Christ Jesus? Here are five misconceptions.

1. **I don't have a "Greater Yes!"**
   Response: You do have a "Greater Yes!" It is part of what it means to be human and created in the image of God.

2. **I have to invent a "Greater Yes!"**
   Response: You do not have to invent your "Greater Yes!" It was planted in you before you were born.

3. **I have a "Greater Yes!", but it's not that important.**
   Response: Your "Greater Yes!" is unique and important. You have been handcrafted by God to accomplish a part of His destiny for the world. Your "Greater Yes!" is meant to fulfill a great need God feels deeply about.

4. **I have a "Greater Yes!", but it's up to God to make it happen.**
   Response: It is your "Greater Yes!" to act on. God is waiting for you to value His gift enough to live for it. He will not force you to choose nor will He make it happen for you. You must choose. You must act. Your "Greater Yes!" is what God has laid hold of you to do.

5. **I had a "Greater Yes!", but it's too late.**
   Response: It is never too late to act. Your "Greater Yes!" is not dead until you are.

Marking Where God Is Moving

The journey requires that you mark where God is moving. He is calling you off your map and onto His compass. You are going to have to listen to and depend only on Him. God told Abraham:

> *Leave your country, your people and your father's household and go to the land I will show you. I will make you into a great nation and I will bless you; I will make your name great, and you will be a blessing. I will bless those who bless you, and whoever curses you I will curse; And all peoples on earth will be blessed through you. So Abram left, as the LORD had told him…and they set out for the land of Canaan…There he built an altar to the LORD and called on the name of the LORD.*
>
> Genesis 12:1–8

As long as Abraham marked where God was moving him and called on him, he stayed on course to God's "Greater Yes!" for him and the generations to come.

The Promise of Your "Greater Yes!"

God has put a driving passion in you to do something special. Why wouldn't he? He created you in His image, and there is no one else exactly like you in the universe. No one else can do your "Greater Yes!"

The way to find that is in your relationship with Christ. You must go after His promise with all of your energy, allowing nothing to deter you or distract you. You must move toward the promise that was instilled with you from the beginning. Maybe you don't know it yet because you've been distracted by making a living instead of a life.

God wants you to do your everyday duties, but he wants you to do them with the understanding of His promise. A lot of promises out there never get met because we don't see them and latch on to them.

The Perspective of Your "Greater Yes!"

God has a God-size vision in you, and it's not about now but about eternity. What are you doing for eternity? As my dad likes to say, eternity is a long time, and what we do on this earth affects our eternity. That is what gets me going in the morning, because I know if I can affect one person, I can affect eternity.

A God-given vision is a God-sized vision, and that always seems overwhelming at first. You may be so overwhelmed by it that you dismiss it from your thinking. But once God puts it in you, it won't let you go until you act on it. Have you been haunted for years by a God-sized vision you've ignored? It's never too late to act on your "Greater Yes!"

I was coaching a wonderful lady one time; she was a trained nurse, but she wanted to go back to school to be a lawyer. When I asked why, she said, "Well, I can make more money." That's not a good enough reason.

Instead, I asked her to consider, "In light of eternity, why would you want to do this?" She took my advice, and now she is going a completely different direction, but in her same field, and I think she's going to be more fulfilled than she's ever been because she is going to live out what God has called her to be.

The Pursuit of Your "Greater Yes!"

Until you decide to pursue your "Greater Yes!", you are never going to live your life the way you were meant to. As soon as you decide you will do what it takes, you are already in pursuit of your dream.

Your "Greater Yes!" may be installing plumbing in houses for the glory of God. I know a guy who has been selling insurance for years and through that has led twenty-six people to Christ in the last two years. He uses the insurance company to meet his "Greater Yes!", which is to win people to Christ.

The Process for Your "Greater Yes!"

If you begin to pursue your "Greater Yes!", God will put you in a process. Because God loves you and is pleased with you, when you pursue His promise and go after your potential and destiny, He will put you in the test. He said to Abraham, "I'm going to make you a great nation," then He put him in the wilderness. He said to Moses, "You're going to set my people free," then He put him and the children of Israel in the desert. Jesus Christ was in the desert for forty days. God will drive us into the desert to be tested by the devil to clarify our calling and refine our character. He simply loves us too much to keep us the way we are.

The Preparation for Your "Greater Yes!"

Your preparation is found in the process, as the journey itself prepares you to succeed at what you were born to be and do.

It's in the desert that God begins to prepare you for your "Greater Yes!" Even Jesus was led into the desert after His baptism (Ma 4). There God prepared Him for His destiny. In some ways, the preparation can be more important than the end result. The journey teaches us it's not about us—it's about God, and the end result will be up to Him.

The Problems Facing Your "Greater Yes!"

Problems always come in the desert, in the midst of the journey. Some of the problems facing the "Greater Yes!" are:

Your comfort zone. We like staying in circumstances that don't demand too much of us. We don't want to get pinched and poked and criticized and evaluated. But the comfort zone is our biggest enemy. A lot of people spend their whole lives preparing for retirement so they can be more comfortable, but that's not what God has called us to do. Retirement is not in the Bible and neither is the idea of creating a comfort zone to hide in.

Your fear. We don't trust God enough because we're looking too much in the mirror and saying, "How are you going to...?" Quite frankly, I would have given up a long time ago because I'm not that talented, gifted, or smart. Overcoming your fear will be a big barrier to living out your "Greater Yes!"

Other people. I can't even count how many people criticized my dad when he packed us all up to move to the Indian reservation. Sometimes you may even find criticism coming from your spouse, your pastor, or a close friend. Use caution and wisdom when considering the opinions of other people, and be careful to move only in God's timing.

The Provision for your "Greater Yes!"

The provision is not about us. [God] *is able to do immeasurably more than all we ask or imagine* (Ep 3:20). You can't even imagine how He will be able to take care of you and what He will do through you. Too many of us find our purpose and then try to figure out how we're going to meet it on our own. We end up saying, "I can't do it; it's humanly impossible."

Don't ask God for a "Greater Yes!" that *you* can do. Ask God for the impossible dream. The other day my wife and I were discussing a ministry opportunity. We both said, "This is impossible. We can't do this." We came to the conclusion, "That's exactly where God wants us." If

we can, He couldn't. The provision is His. There is an incredible resource of power and provision within each of us who have accepted
Christ. When we receive Christ in our lives, we automatically receive
the power of the Holy Spirit indwelling us. All we have to do is plug
into that power. It is our choice.

The Purpose of Your "Greater Yes!"

Most Christians will never see the big picture of why God put them
on this earth. You can spend a whole lifetime just marking the days instead of making a life and accomplishing the great thing He has for
you, what you were destined to do.

It's not too late; you can invest the rest of your life in a "Greater
Yes!" Simply get on your knees before God and ask Him, "What do
you want me to do with my life?" It's up to you to make the choice.
What are you destined to become?

The Power of Your "Greater Yes!"

The power of your "Greater Yes!" is found in your relationship with
Christ and by plugging into the power of the Holy Spirit that dwells
within you. It's found in that deep, intimate understanding of who He
is. The more I get to know God, the more I get to know myself. The
more I get to know Jesus Christ as my friend and the one who loves
me more than I love myself, the more I get to know what my dream
is and what I'm capable of doing.

The Potential of Your "Greater Yes!"

What are you destined to become? You can realize your God-given potential. You can define, discover, develop, and deploy your fingerprint
of potential and destiny (Ep 2:10).

I don't fear failure. I fear succeeding at the things that don't matter.
We have an incredible potential to see God do amazing things through
us. What kind of impression do you want to leave on this temporal
world and on eternity? The choice is yours.

The good news for your "Greater Yes!" is that each stage or obstacle
along your journey is intended not to block but to help you break
through to the fulfillment of God's potential and destiny for your life.
The way is difficult, but anything less is not living at all! Keep marking
where God is moving, and you will find your potential and destiny.

Imagine the possibilities!

MOVING TOWARD YOUR "GREATER YES!"

1. Think back to what you wanted to do while you were growing up, and write a short description of it and why it appealed to you.

2. Interview three people you respect, who you think are living out their "Greater Yes!"

3. If someone came along and gave you all the time, talent, treasure, and talent you ever needed, what would you do with it?

4. Observe your life and write down your conclusions.

   • What have you always been good at?

   • What needs do you care about most?

   • Whom do you admire most and why?

   • What makes you feel most fulfilled?

   • What do you love to do most?

   • What have you felt called to do?

5. What legacy would you like to leave for your children and grandchildren?

6. What are you willing to sacrifice?

7. How could you mobilize your family to help you pursue your "Greater Yes?"

8. To what degree will you use obstacles as excuses?

9. Is there anything you can do right now to launch you toward your "Greater Yes?"

10. What does your family feel or think about your "Greater Yes!"

MY PRAYER OF COMMITMENT

Father, thank You for the journey You have me on. I know it is all part of the process to help me realize and experience my potential and destiny for my life. Give me the insight and wisdom to move toward defining, discovering, developing and deploying my "Greater Yes!" Thank You that I can live a life that echoes in eternity. Amen!

CHAPTER 31

Unpacking Your Lunch

God has given each of us a lunch—it's time to give it to him!

The little boy in John 6 had a lunch to give. He had five loaves and two fish. When he unpacked it and willingly gave it to Jesus, a miracle happened. He was not responsible for performing the miracle; he was only to give his lunch. It is time to unpack your "Greater Yes!" and imagine the miracles God could do through you.

This chapter is meant to help you unpack the lunch that God has given you. This lunch makes up your "Greater Yes!"—your God-given potential and destiny. Consider getting away on a personal retreat or with a group of friends and spend at least a day working through this as you unpack your lunch.

Discovering Your "Greater Yes!"

In your search for your "Greater Yes!", consider the following questions:

- What is God showing you that can only be seen through the eyes of your heart?
- What is God laying on your heart that could only have come from Him?
- What is God showing you that is breaking His heart?
- What has God put in your heart that causes your heart to break?
- What is God creating in you that could only have come from and be accomplished by Him?
- How has God used you in the past and how does He want to use you now?
- What kind of legacy do you want to leave behind that will echo in eternity?

Individual Exercises

The following exercises are designed to provide you with insights you can utilize in discovering your "Greater Yes!"

Case Study: Nehemiah's Vision

Please read the following case study about a heroic Biblical figure who got a "Greater Yes!" and changed the course of Jewish history. There are reflection questions at the end to help you further understand this example.

The year was 445 BC, and Nehemiah was the grandson of a Hebrew exile and the cupbearer to King Artaxerxes of Persia.

One day he met his brother and others who had just returned from Jerusalem. The report he got broke his heart—the restoration of Jerusalem and the Temple, approved and commissioned by the previous Persian king Cyrus, had been halted by a decree of King Artaxerxes. Not only had reconstruction been halted, but new construction was leveled and burned. For the next four months, Nehemiah prayed and fasted for his countrymen living in Jerusalem. He became convinced that he was to lead in the rebuilding of Jerusalem's walls.

He devised a plan and asked God for success. No visitor was to be in the King's presence unless that visitor was upbeat and positive, but on this day Artaxerxes noticed that Nehemiah looked sad. Nehemiah didn't know what the King would do. Would he punish Nehemiah, demote him, or show him mercy?

When the King asked why his face was sad, Nehemiah replied, *"May the King live forever! Why should my face not look sad when the city where my fathers are buried lies in ruins, and its gates have been destroyed by fire?"* (Ne 2:3). The King responded, "What is it you want?" (v. 4).

Nehemiah asked that Artaxerxes send him to Jerusalem to rebuild it. He also asked for letters guaranteeing him safety on the trip and access to the King's forest. The King's only question was *How long will your journey take, and when will you get back?* (v. 6). God's hand of grace was extended to Nehemiah, and he went on his way. Artaxerxes even provided an escort.

Upon arrival, Nehemiah met with both opposition and a city in shambles. His first task was to scope out the size of the job. He then enlisted the residents to begin again to rebuild the walls by sharing with them Artaxerxes' letters and his verbal blessing. He divided up the work among the families with each having a specific section to build.

The work began, but so did the opposition, creating fear among the people. They had been stopped before and their work destroyed. So they prayed and developed a plan. Half the men would work while the other half stood guard, equipped with spears, shields, bows, and armor. If one area was attacked, the trumpet would call the others to their defense.

The wall was completed in fifty-two days. It was a testimony to Nehemiah's leadership and vision, but more importantly, it sent a strong message to the enemies of Israel that the wall had been built with the help of their God. Nehemiah led the people in a great celebration with songs, music, dancing, and praise to God.

Nehemiah ruled the people, paying attention to the poor, avoiding the perks of the "governor" role, and eliminating the harsh tax system. In league with Ezra, Nehemiah instituted reforms that brought about repentance and changes in the behavior of the people.

In the year 432 BC, twenty-six years after gaining permission to rebuild Jerusalem, Nehemiah, true to his commitment, returned to the service of Artaxerxes.

Reflection Questions
1. What was it that broke Nehemiah's heart?
2. What was his response?
3. What became his "Greater Yes!"?
4. What obstacles stood in his way?
5. What were the things that made his vision a reality?
6. In what ways did his "Greater Yes!" grow during the twenty-six years he was in Jerusalem?

Please keep Nehemiah in mind as you complete the following exercises designed to help you move toward discovering your "Greater Yes!"

Life Experiences
- What satisfying experiences have provided you joy, energy, and a desire to experience more?
- What unsatisfying experiences have robbed you of your joy, energy, and which you hope never to experience again?
- How has God used you in any of these experiences to glorify Him, bless others, or contribute to His kingdom on earth?

Strengths
- What skills, activities, and behaviors come naturally or have you developed to a high level? (Example: public speaking)

Non-Strengths
- What activities and behaviors are difficult for you to accomplish? (Example: administrative tasks)

Talents
- What things do you and others recognize that you do well but that you would not describe as strengths?

Spiritual Gifts (1 Corinthians 12:28–31)
- Spiritual gifts are your activities and behaviors that God uses on an on-going basis to bless others and build His kingdom. What are your spiritual gifts? How and in what contexts are you are using these gifts now?

Today's Realities
- What is God already doing around you that you feel good about and can support? Example: Ongoing ministries or activities that you may or may not be a part of.
- What are you already doing that God might want you to expand your involvement with or formalize your participation in? Could it potentially become part of His "Greater Yes!" for your life?
- What fear(s) or belief(s) are blocking you from believing that God can and wants to utilize you for His kingdom?
- What obligations do you have that must be taken into consideration when determining your "Greater Yes!" (Example: Obligations to spouse, family, aging parents, etc.)
- What has God prompted you to do that you have avoided to this point?

Passion
Described as zealous, God-given energy that propels you toward achieving your "Greater Yes!", this God-given passion is given to those who have "eyes to see and ears to hear."
- What has God put on your heart that causes your heart to "glow" or "break"?
- What is God showing you that is breaking His heart?
- What is God laying on your heart that could only have come from Him?
- What is God asking you to do that only He can do through you?
- Do you have a "Life Scripture" passage that has provided guidance or comfort? If so, what does it suggest to you about your passion or perhaps God's passion for His creation?

Legacy

A legacy may be a worldview, behaviors or character traits, lifestyle, business or ministry left behind for the benefits of those who come after you.

- **Past:** What legacy have you created in the way you have lived in the past ten years?
- **Present:** What legacy are you creating now? How would those who know you best describe your present legacy?
- **Future:** What legacy do you want to leave?

Great Ideas Blitz

Review your answers to the questions above. Brainstorm as many great ideas for things that could potentially be part of a "Greater Yes!" for your life. For this exercise, imagine you have no restraints or lack of resources to accomplish any of these ideas. (If you prefer to draw a picture, please do so.)

"Greater Yes!" Statement

- It is a verbal picture of God's specific calling on your life. It can be stated in a few words.
- It defines success or significance as you understand it for your life. This may include personal qualities you want to be remembered for, contributions you want to make, accomplishments you want to achieve.
- It provides focus, direction, and a basis for making life's decisions.
- It describes "who you are" and your "place in life."
- It defines your role(s) in your current or future desired life state.
- It is often quite broad or very specific.

Examples

- "I am an apprentice servant leader in the kingdom of God."
- "To live my life as husband, father and businessman in a manner that glorifies God and brings joy to myself and those around me"
- "I will feed the hungry."
- "I will build a business that funds ministry around the world."
- "I want to build a lodge that becomes a place of healing for pastors and missionaries."

Exercise

- Write your own "Greater Yes!" statement using as few words as necessary.

- Take your time. Review answers to the questions above. Consider your statement a draft. Write down your thoughts as fast as they come to you.

Steps for Making Your "Greater Yes!" a Reality

Making your "Greater Yes!" a living reality is the objective. Words on paper never change lives. Words written on the heart do. The goal is to have a God-breathed "Greater Yes!" and a plan to which you are passionately committed.

Step 1: Pray over each word of your statement. Let the Holy Spirit be your editor. Ask for guidance in completing the remainder of the steps.

Step 2: Share your "Greater Yes!" with your spouse. She/he needs to be able to support your vision. If that's not possible, you may have to negotiate a vision that is not only acceptable but can be blessed by your spouse.

Step 3: Share your "Greater Yes!" with your small group, accountability partner and others you trust. Ask for feedback, both positive and negative, throughout the process.

Step 4: Create a "Master's Plan" consisting of the following:
- Specific, measurable, time-bounded and doable goals.
- Obstacles to the plan by goal and ways for overcoming them.
- Resources you need to make your plan work. Begin living each day as if the plan were completed. Each day, give your "Greater Yes!" and your plans back to God. Ask for continued guidance. Celebrate every milestone, and give praise to your Editor-in-Chief.

You can live a life that echoes in eternity!

Developing Your "Greater Yes!"

There are some essentials you need to consider when allowing God to develop your "Greater Yes!" in and through you. Reflect on the related questions.

1. God is asking you to trust Him enough to risk it all.
   Who or what is keeping you from moving out, pressing on, risking it all?
2. God is more concerned about what He is doing in you than with or through you.
   What is God trying to do in you that is preventing you from reach-

ing your potential and destiny? Do you need to focus on His work IN you in order to clear the path for what He wants you to do?

3. God wants to create in you a higher level of dependency.
   What or who are you depending on to provide the resources you need?

4. God will always meet you at your level of expectancy
   If you had unlimited resources and complete freedom to fail, what would you attempt for God?

5. God wants to turn your thoughts and words into power for your potential.
   What thoughts or words are keeping you or others from their potential or destiny?

6. God allows adversities and difficulties in your life according to your need.
   How do you view or how do you respond to your adversities and difficulties?

7. God wants you plugging into the power that is already within you.
   How are you getting plugged into the power of the Holy Spirit within you?

You can live a life that stands out rather than blends in!

Deploying Your "Greater Yes!"

Getting It Going

This is where many get stuck—the actual implementation of the "Greater Yes!" Many have an idea and a passion for their call but do not have the faith for it. There is a stretching and a lack of control that is uncomfortable. God never said you would be comfortable.

Some people are waiting for the perfect plan before they get started. But remember, a great plan with no action will get you nowhere while a poor plan with great action will get you towards your destination. You do not have all of the pieces to the puzzle. You could not handle the entire plan if it were presented at once. Have faith in the one who gave you your "Greater Yes!" Don't worry about making the perfect decision, just move on what you know and trust God. Consider the following:

- What can you do now?
- What may have to wait?

- Have you shared your "Greater Yes!" with others?
- Do you have someone to keep you accountable?
- Are you praying about your "Greater Yes!" daily?

Think Process

What systems need to be put in place to realize and deploy your "Greater Yes!"? The following are some general guidelines of the processes for achieving your "Greater Yes!"

- Cover it with prayer. Every part and every aspect needs prayer and people to partner with you in prayer.
- Write a vision/mission statement. This tool will help keep you focused on where you are going.
- Find partners. Who do you need to join you and assist you on the way?
- Determine size. Will you need to be incorporated or will you be doing the same work with new principles?
- Determine shortfall. What do you currently find lacking in the completion of the "Greater Yes!"?
- Cast the vision. This is a way of gaining support, accountability, awareness, and partners.
- Make goals. Create lists of goals for six months, one year, five years, and ten years.
- Be open to God's leading. God will take you places you do not expect to go.

Leadership

Your "Greater Yes!" will never be realized without qualified leadership. Everything rises and falls on the competency of you and your leadership team. Here are some questions for you to consider.

- What kind of leader do you need to be?
- What kind of leadership is needed to carry out your "Greater Yes!"?
- How can you go about building a leadership team?
- Can you become a leader who can cast vision?
- You will need leadership that brings strength in your area of weakness.
- Find servant leaders.

Obstacles

An obstacle is anything that could prevent us from fulfilling our "Greater Yes!" To consider these is not to foster doubt but to build a realistic plan. We have to consider all that may come between us and the goal. Obstacles become opportunities to trust and depend on God. Here are some obstacles to consider:

- Time. Excluding work, what absorbs most of your time? Is there any situation, if changed, which would give you more time? Could someone help you free up time? Are you prioritizing your time?
- Finances. Have you broken down the cost into sections or steps and started at the first piece? Can you adjust your lifestyle to aid in the requirements of this need?
- Skills. Can you learn the required skills that are missing? If so, can you learn them from the experience of the journey or do you need some training?
- Location. Is there a better location? What would be gained by a different location? Can you start in your current location? What about your current location is hindering you? What is keeping you there?

Budget

A budget is needed for any size of call. What will have to be given and sacrificed in order to fulfill your "Greater Yes!"? Looking at a big budget for a citywide event may be too much for many of us to comprehend. However, if you generate a cost for each portion of the event, it becomes more manageable. Look at the small portions, even if you have to make some guesses. It will be closer than you imagine. Just be sure to hit every detail you can think of (this is where brainstorming with others helps).

- Break down each component and come up with cost. Guess if necessary.
- Will there be a different cost in the future? Can you anticipate it? Can you prepare for it?
- How will you fund it? Will your resources come from you or will you ask others?
- What will happen if you do not have enough funds for the budget? Do you have an alternate plan?
- Do you have a routine for reexamination of the budget?
- Prepare to see God's hand.

Evaluate and Adjust

Routinely evaluate the progress of your "Greater Yes!" The journey is a living thing. God is more interested in what happens inside of you than what is getting done. He will also reveal new things to you and others with you. These revelations can take you down a different path. That is okay; remember whose "Greater Yes!" it is anyway.

- Keep your "Greater Yes!" before God and you.
- Reexamine progress of goals.
- Reexamine progress of budget.
- Make adjustments as needed.

Be Ready to Fly

This is a new place for you. If you are moving toward the place God has called you, you obviously are not there yet. You must expect things to change, and you must be willing to change. How could you expect to be at a different place without any change from where you are now? These changes will call you off your map and onto God's compass. That is where the growth is and where He wants you, in total dependence on Him. Here are some things you need to examine:

- Are you ready for the thrill of a lifetime?
- Is anything holding you back?
- Day to day, where is your focus?
- Do you have an accountability partner, team, or coach?
- Do you know anyone who has been where you are going?
- Is there any reason you should not get going?

Live your life so loudly that others want to hear your words!

My son Doug once said, "We should never be surprised, but always amazed." I think that is good advice. We should be amazed by the grace and mercy of God that He should love us in our condition and call us to unimaginable opportunities when we learn to exchange our many lesser yeses for that one "Greater Yes!"

ENJOY YOUR LIFE OF SIGNIFICANCE!!!

Imagine the Possibilities!

NOTES

Chapter 7:
[1]John Ortberg, *If You Want to Walk on Water, You've Got to Get Out of the Boat* (Grand Rapids: Zondervan, 2001), 71.

Chapter 13:
[1]From a sermon by Pastor Doug Brown, Lee's Summit Community Church, 2005.

Chapter 22:
[1]Candace Savage, *Eagles of North America* (Ashland, WI: NorthWord, Inc., 2000).

Chapter 23:
[1]Joel Osteen, *Your Best Life Now: 7 Steps to Living at Your Full Potential* (New York: Warner Faith, 2004), 143-144.

Chapter 26:
[1]Erwin Raphael McManus, *Seizing Your Divine Moment* (Nashville: Thomas Nelson, 2002), 38-39.

Chapter 27:
[1]Winston S. Churchill, ed. *Never Give in: The Best of Winston Churchill Speeches* (New York: Hyperion, 2003), 306.

ABOUT THE AUTHOR

Dr. Dan Erickson is a product of a missionary's home, and has received a Bachelor's of Science, Master's of Divinity and Doctor of Ministry degrees. His doctoral work focused on leadership development.

Dan's leadership background includes extensive pastoral ministry experience of more than thirty years in five dynamic churches, overseeing adult and children education, small groups, singles, men's ministries and pastoral interns. He has additional experience as an Executive Pastor and a professional life coach.

While pastoring, Dan filled the roles of Executive Vice President and Academic Dean of the Northwest Graduate School Doctor of Ministry program. In the past several years, he has served as National Director of Denominational and Parachurch Relations with Promise Keepers and Executive Vice President of Ministry Advancement for the National Coalition of Men's Ministries (NCMM). Dan is currently Associate Pastor of Lee's Summit Community Church and the Chief Servant Leader of People Matter Ministries, a ministry seeking to help individuals, churches and ministries see their potential become reality through coaching, consulting, writing, and speaking.

Dan met his wife Cathy while attending college. They have been married for 35 years and have two children and four grandchildren. Cathy is currently directing "Step UP," a ministry to single mothers and their children. Step UP gives single-mom families an opportunity to break the cycle of past hurts, strengthen the family during challenging times, and prepare a positive, uplifting path to their future.

ABOUT PEOPLE MATTER MINISTRIES

Purpose…

"To help people discover, develop, and deploy their fingerprint of potential"

"There are no ordinary people."

—C.S. Lewis

We believe…
- People are created in the image of God with *dignity and worth*.
- People are God's and mankind's *most valuable resource*.
- People are individuals who are *"Uniquely You."*
- People can discover, develop and deploy their own *"Fingerprint of Potential."*
- People discover and develop their greatest potential in the context of a *safe and trusting environment*.
- People are best served and deployed when led by *"Servant Leaders."*

Through responsible leadership, we will …
- Honor God in all we do and say.
- Provide motivation with vision and purpose.
- Provide expertise with a commitment to integrity and service.
- Promote and celebrate uniqueness and diversity.
- Be careful listeners, faithful stewards, and consistent examples.

"My greatest fear is not failure; it is succeeding at something that does not matter."

New Tribes Missionary,
Author Unknown

General Information:

Mailing Address:
816 NE Chestnut St.
Lee's Summit, MO 64086

Phone: 816.554.8169
Email: Derickson@peoplematterministries.com
Email: Cerickson@peoplematterministries.com
Website: www.peoplematterministries.com
Website: www.thegreateryes.com

Ministries:

Finding Your Greater Yes! Conference
Contact: Dr. Dan Erickson
Voice: 816.554.8169
Email: *derickson@peoplematterministries.com*

Empowering Men Conference
Contact: Rex Tignor
Voice: 804.382.5671
Email: *mensministriesofva@comcast.net*

Step UP Ministry to Single Mothers
Contact: Cathy Erickson
Singles Second Wind Conference
Sheri Hern
Voice: 816.524.6786 Ext. 140
Email: *cerickson@peoplematterministries.com*

RECOMMENDED READING

Lucado, Max. *Cure for the Common Life* (Nashville: W Publishing Group, 2005).

McManus, Erwin Raphael. *Seizing Your Divine Moment* (Nashville: Thomas Nelson, 2002).

Osteen, Joel. *Your Best Life Now: 7 Steps to Living at Your Full Potential* (New York: Warner Faith, 2004).

Warren, Rick. *Purpose Driven Life* (Grand Rapids: Zondervan, 2002).

Wilkinson, Bruce. *The Dream Giver* (Sisters, OR: Multnomah Publishers, 2003).